TOP 10
TORONTO

Top 10 Toronto Highlights

The Top 10 of Everything

CONTENTS

Toronto Area by Area

Streetsmart

Within each Top 10 list in this book, no hierarchy of quality or popularity is implied. All 10 are, in the editor's opinion, of roughly equal merit.
 Throughout this book, floors are referred to in accordance with American usage; i.e., the "first floor" is at ground level.

Title page, front cover and spine
Toronto's impressive skyscrapers at dusk
Back cover, clockwise from top left *Aerial view of Niagara Falls; kayaking in Toronto Harbourfront; Nathan Phillips Square; skyline of Toronto; Gooderham Flatiron building*

Welcome to
Toronto

Renowned museums and eclectic galleries; fine dining and cozy bistros; cobblestones and cutting-edge architecture; elegant department stores and quirky shops; a medieval-style castle with secret passageways; Niagara Falls within striking distance. Toronto is a city of contrasts, and with Eyewitness Top 10 Toronto it's yours to explore.

Toronto is a thriving metropolis that's home to one of the world's most multicultural populations. It has a contemporary vibe, yet the city is filled with historic treasures. The cobblestoned **Distillery Historic District** blends Victorian architecture with boutiques, galleries, and restaurants. The **St. Lawrence Market**, named the world's best market by *National Geographic* magazine, has been operating as a food emporium since 1803.

As for the city's modern-day persona, the safe, exciting downtown area has striking skyscrapers, fabulous shopping at the **CF Eaton Centre**, an array of family attractions such as the **Ripley's Aquarium of Canada**, and – honoring Canada's national pastime – the **Hockey Hall of Fame**. **Harbourfront**, stretching along Lake Ontario, provides hours of browsing pleasure. Catch the ferry here for the short sail to the scenic **Toronto Islands**.

Whether you're visiting for a weekend or a week, our Top 10 guide brings together the best of everything that Toronto has to offer, from the **Art Gallery of Ontario**'s outstanding collection of fine art and modern sculpture to **Casa Loma**'s architectural grandeur. This guide has useful tips throughout, from seeking out what's free to avoiding the crowds, plus seven easy-to-follow itineraries designed to tie together a clutch of sights in a short space of time. Add inspiring photography and detailed maps, and you've got the essential pocket-sized travel companion. **Enjoy the book, and enjoy Toronto.**

Clockwise from top: **Toronto skyline, Art Gallery of Ontario, Ripley's Aquarium, Niagara Falls,** *Our Game* **sculpture in the Hockey Hall of Fame, National Bay Islands, Distillery Historic District**

Exploring Toronto

Toronto offers a mosaic of attractions. These suggestions for a two- and four-day stay are designed so that visitors to the city can experience Toronto's most popular places in a short space of time. Many of the destinations are close to each other, so it's easy to mix and match. It's a good idea to pick a clear, sunny day for a visit to CN Tower.

Ripley's Aquarium is home to a kaleidoscope of marine life.

Two Days in Toronto

Day ❶
MORNING
Head up the **CN Tower** (see pp16–17) for an incredible view of the city, the lake, and beyond. Then visit **Ripley's Aquarium** (see pp28–9) and check out some extraordinary marine life.
AFTERNOON
Walk to **Harbourfront** (see pp66–9) along Queens Quay. Take the ferry to the **Toronto Islands** (see pp18–19), and enjoy the activities and the views.

Day ❷
MORNING
Start at **Union Station** (see p45) and go up Bay Street, past the skyscrapers and the Romanesque-style **Old City Hall** (see p78). Head to **CF Toronto Eaton Centre** (see pp30–31) to shop.
AFTERNOON
Take the Bay bus north to **Bloor Street** (see p79), and have lunch in the Yorkville area. There are plenty of good choices on Cumberland Street and Yorkville Avenue. Walk

Key
— Two-day itinerary
— Four-day itinerary

to the **Royal Ontario Museum** (see pp12–13) and enjoy the permanent collection and featured exhibition. Take a short cab ride or the subway (Museum station) north to **Casa Loma** (see pp24–5), exiting at Dupont station and then climb the stairs to the Gothic castle on the hill.

Four Days in Toronto

Day ❶
MORNING
Explore **Fort York** (see p68), Canada's largest collection of buildings from the War of 1812 era, then head to the

Around Toronto

CN Tower (see pp16–17) and **Ripley's Aquarium** (see pp28–9) to view what's under the sea.

AFTERNOON

Walk eastward along Front Street to **Union Station** (see p45). Gaze up at the bank buildings. Continue north along Bay Street to **Old City Hall** (see p78), before indulging in some exciting retail therapy at the **CF Toronto Eaton Centre** (see pp30–31).

Day ❷
MORNING

Explore the **Hockey Hall of Fame** (see pp32–3) then walk eastward to **St. Lawrence Market** (see p90). Later, continue east to the **Distillery Historic District** (see pp26–7), for its galleries, boutiques, and cafés.

AFTERNOON

From the Distillery, catch the 121 bus westbound, exiting at Blue Jay Way. Alongside the lake, at **Harbourfront** (see pp66–9), stop off to visit the **Power Plant Contemporary Art Gallery** (see p70). Catch the ferry to the **Toronto Islands** (see pp18–19) for a picnic.

Day ❸
MORNING

Visit **Niagara Falls** (see pp34–7) and, weather permitting, take a boat tour with Hornblower Cruises.

AFTERNOON

Visit the **Niagara Falls Butterfly Conservatory** (see p35), then head to

Kensington Market offers an array of colorful shops and wares.

the **Niagara-on-the-Lake** (see p101). If time allows, dine one of the town's fine restaurants and see a play at the Shaw Festival in summer.

Day ❹
MORNING

Visit the **Art Gallery of Ontario** (see pp20–21), with its collections of Canadian and European art. Wander through **Chinatown** (see p77) and **Kensington Market** (see p75). Both areas offer excellent lunch options.

AFTERNOON

Explore the **Royal Ontario Museum** (see pp12–13). Afterwards, take a short cab ride or hop on the subway at Museum station and head north to **Casa Loma** (see pp24–5), exiting at Dupont and climbing the stairs to the Gothic castle.

Casa Loma stands on a hill keeping a watchful eye over downtown.

Top 10 Toronto Highlights

The spectacular Horseshoe Falls roaring over the cliff at Niagara Falls

Top 10 Toronto Highlights

As Canada's largest city and its financial hub, Toronto has a tremendous amount to offer, with a thriving arts scene, top museums, world-class restaurants and shops, and a beautiful lakeside location with lovely beaches. The city's cultural diversity, with over 90 ethnic groups, makes it a vibrant and exciting urban center.

Royal Ontario Museum

A treasure-trove of ancient mummies, exquisitely decorated period rooms, huge dinosaurs, stuffed birds, stunning Chinese art, and imposing Greek and Roman sculptures are among the many rewarding sights to be seen during a visit to this museum *(see pp12–15)*.

CN Tower and its Views

High-speed external elevators mounted on one of the tallest buildings in the Western Hemisphere will whisk you up 181 stories to an unforgettable view of the city *(see pp16–17)*.

Toronto Islands

A short ferry ride from downtown, this chain of small islands provides a respite from summer heat with its beaches, picnic grounds, and amusement park *(see pp18–19)*.

Art Gallery of Ontario

This fabulous museum is home to an excellent collection of Canadian art, including that of contemporary artist Michael Snow. There are also fine collections of French Impressionists, Inuit art, sculpture, photography, and prints *(see pp20–21)*.

Casa Loma

Built by financier Sir Henry Pellatt, this turreted mansion, with grand rooms and beautiful gardens, offers a glimpse of turn-of-the-20th-century luxury *(see pp24–5)*.

6 Distillery Historic District ✓

Once the largest distillery in North America, this complex is one of Toronto's hottest destinations. Victorian buildings and cobblestoned streets provide a backdrop to the many unusual stores and galleries, and lovely restaurants and cafés found here (see pp26–7).

7 Ripley's Aquarium of Canada

Greet sharks, octopuses, stingrays, and giant grouper in this impressive aquarium. Start with the Canadian Waters gallery, home to four over-70-year-old lobsters (see pp28–9).

8 CF Toronto Eaton Centre

Toronto's pre-eminent downtown mall, named after a now-defunct department-store chain, is located near major hotels and attractions. If you are looking for a one-stop shopping destination, this mall is it (see pp30–31).

9 Hockey Hall of Fame ✗

Most visitors to Toronto who are ice-hockey fans make a pilgrimage here to see the original Stanley Cup, shoot pucks at a video goalie, walk through a re-created locker room, and watch some of hockey's sterling moments in the Broadcast Zone (see pp32–3).

10 Niagara Falls

After the 2-hour drive from Toronto, stand on Table Rock for a look at one of the world's wonders, the magnificent Horseshoe Falls, where the Niagara River plunges over a 188-ft (57-m) precipice. The town of Niagara Falls and the outlying area offer fine dining, entertainment, winery tours, museums, and more (see pp34–7).

ORKVILLE
BAY STREET
YONGE STREET
JARVIS STREET
CARLTON ST
BAY STREET
DUNDAS ST EAST
8 DOWNTOWN
QUEEN STREET EAST
YONGE
JARVIS
KING STREET EAST
9
6
HARBOURFRONT

Toronto Inner Harbour

0 meters 800
0 yards 800

TOP 10 ⭐ Royal Ontario Museum

The Royal Ontario Museum, or ROM, was created in 1914 with the dual mandate of showcasing human civilization and the natural world. It is now Canada's largest museum, with over six million objects. Galleries of archeology, science, art, world cultures, and natural history display collections of Chinese treasures, mummy cases, and dinosaur skeletons. Hands-on exhibits invite kids to excavate for fossils and examine species under a microscope.

1 Futalognkosaurus Dinosaur

A dinosaur so big that he wouldn't fit inside the main exhibition hall. The Futalognkosaurus (right) greets visitors as they enter the museum lobby.

2 Acropolis Model

This model of Greek temple life depicts the Parthenon and other buildings as they looked at the height of ancient Greek civilization.

3 Totem Poles

Four striking totem poles were carved out of western red cedar in the 1880s by the Haida and the Nisga'a peoples of Canada's northwest coast. The tallest is over 80 ft (24 m) high.

4 Djedmaatesankh Mummy

Decorated with hieroglyphics, this Egyptian sarcophagus (left), dating from c.850 BC, has the mummified body of a female court musician. It has never been opened, but a CAT scan revealed that she died aged 35 from a tooth abscess.

5 Chinese Guardian Lions

Two proud stone lions, which were carved for a Beijing palace in the 1600s, stand guard outside the museum.

NEED TO KNOW

MAP C3 ▪ 100 Queen's Park (the main entrance is around the corner on Bloor St W) ▪ 416 586 8000 ▪ www.rom.on.ca

Open 10am–5:30pm daily (check website for Mon)

Adm $20 adults, $17 senior citizens, $16.50 students, $14 children aged 4–14; separate adm fee for special exhibitions; adm free third Mon of month 5:30–8:30pm

▪ The Royal Ontario Museum is located very close to St. George and Museum subway stations.

▪ Visitors can grab a quick bite in the cafeteria on Basement Level 1.

▪ Most of the special programming on the website is free.

6 Living Beehive

This active beehive is a highlight of the Hands-On Biodiversity Gallery. See the interior of the hive, buzzing with honey bees that have flown in from outdoors.

Floor Plan of Royal Ontario Museum

Key to Floor Plan
- Level 1
- Level 2
- Level 3

9 Mosaic Dome

A spectacular mosaic dome **(right)** tops the rotunda. Over a million tiny colored squares of Venetian glass form symbols of ancient cultures, such as an Inca thunder god and a mythical Greek seahorse.

10 English Parlor

Dating from the 1750s, with original carved pine walls and furniture, this parlor looks as if a wealthy gentleman and his card-playing friends have only momentarily left the room. Though the gilded harp in the corner is silent, some evocative, ambient Baroque music completes the vignette.

7 Hardwood Forest

The dappled light and hushed calm of an Ontario hardwood forest are perfectly re-created in this diorama. If you look closely, you will see more than 20 animals, among them a porcupine and fox.

8 Ming Tomb

Guarded by stone camels, a fierce warrior, and a scepter-bearing adviser, this ensemble of funerary sculpture **(below)** features artifacts from the Yuan dynasty (1271–1368), Ming dynasty (1368–1644), as well as Qing dynasty (1644–1912).

MUSEUM GUIDE

Walkways on each level join exhibitions in the Michael Lee-Chin Crystal to the main building. Level 1 includes the Korea, China, and Japan collections, and galleries exploring Canada's First Peoples and Canadian heritage. Natural history is the focus of Level 2, with galleries on gems and minerals, evolution, and dinosaurs. Level 3 features anthropology and archeology, with artifacts from Africa, the Americas, Asia Pacific, Egypt, and Rome, as well as 20th-century art and design. Textiles as well as the Institute for Contemporary Culture are on Level 4.

Royal Ontario Museum Collections

Paallirmiut clothing, Canada's First Peoples

1 Dinosaurs
The Dinosaur Gallery, on Level 2 in the Michael Lee-Chin Crystal, is home to around 25 dinosaur skeletons of both marine and land dwellers. This includes the world's most complete *Maiasaura* and her baby, which are thought to be 80 million years old.

2 Hands-On Biodiversity
Get up close with the wonders of the natural world in this imaginative discovery zone on Level 2. Touch animal skulls and pelts, and don special glasses to look at the world through the "eyes" of animals.

Egyptian wall-cast sculpture

3 Ancient Egypt
More than 1,000 artifacts, from gold earrings to ceremonial mummy cases, combine to shed more light on ancient Egypt (Level 3). A plaster cast taken from the temple of Queen Hatsheput near present-day Somalia, provides an opportunity to test your skill at decoding hieroglyphics.

4 Arms and Armor
On Level 3, battle gear stands guard over some 300 pieces – from 15th-century European chain mail to World War I automatic weapons – that show the history of human conflict.

5 Canada's First Peoples
The ROM's holdings of indigenous artifacts, on Level 1, are superb. National treasures include an Innu-painted caribou-skin coat and a quilled pouch collected by Canadian painter Paul Kane (1810–71), who traveled among indigenous settlements in the mid-1800s. Don't miss the Umiak boat, which is large enough to hold an entire village.

6 Ice Age Mammals
The rise of mammals following the Ice Age's "big chill," which ended about 10,000 years ago, is explored in this dramatic exhibit on Level 2. A giant beaver, mastodon, saber-toothed cat, and hippopotamus are just some of the impressive specimens on display.

7 Gallery of Birds
Hundreds of birds from all over the world swoop together in one spectacular flock, suspended in mid-flight from the ceiling on Level 2. Marvel at the 9-ft- (2.7-m-) wing span of the albatross; listen to birdsongs at interactive booths; and pull out drawers containing nests, bones, eggs, and feathers.

8 Art Deco
Rare French and American Art Deco furniture, lamps, and sculpture (exquisitely crafted from ebony, lacquer, and ivory, among other fine materials) celebrate this influential design movement of the 1920s and 1930s. Art Deco glass, ceramic, and silver pieces round out this collection, on Level 3.

9 Greek Sculpture
Striking stone, bronze, and ivory sculptures make this collection on Level 3 one of the best in North

America. The pieces dating back to the Hellenistic Age, around 325 BC, reflect the development of Greek society under Alexander the Great, as his army forged into Egypt and India.

10 Chinese Art

Spanning over 6,000 years of Chinese history (4500 BC to AD 1900), this collection on Level 1 ranks among the world's finest. The procession of 7th-century ceramic tomb figures and the monumental Buddhist sculptures from the 12th to the 16th centuries are outstanding.

Ceramic figures, Chinese art gallery

THE CRYSTAL

The highlight of the museum's renovation is the Michael Lee-Chin Crystal, a magnificent addition designed by world-renowned architect Daniel Libeskind and named for the lead donor. This jagged crystalline structure of interlocking forms, with its spectacular atrium space, glass-sliver windows, and jutting angles thrusting over the sidewalk, now forms the dramatic entrance to the museum. Inside the Crystal, which has been designed to have no right angles, are four levels of galleries, including two unusual spaces: the Spirit House, a soaring void crisscrossed by bridges linking the newer galleries, and the Stair of Wonders, an intriguing vertical cabinet of curiosities from the ROM's collection. The Crystal is linked on all levels except the fourth to the original building.

The Royal Ontario Museum building is an engaging fusion of traditional and modern.

TOP 10 ARCHITECTURAL HIGHLIGHTS

1 Rotunda

2 Totem Poles

3 Queen's Park facade

4 Stained-glass windows, Queen's Park entrance

5 Spirit House

6 Liza's Garden

7 Floor mosaic at the entrance to Samuel European Galleries

8 Leaded windows in the stairwells

9 Arched windows along the western facade

10 Exterior cornice around the building

TOP 10 ⭐ CN Tower and its Views

A 58-second elevator ride whisks you to the 114th story of one of the tallest buildings in the Western Hemisphere, the 181-story, 1,815-ft (553-m) communications tower built by Canadian National Railway in 1976. Views from the glass-fronted elevator set the stage for more dizzying sights from the LookOut, where visitors can walk on the Glass Floor for a view 1,122 ft (342 m) straight down. For panoramic views 1,465 ft (447 m) above the ground, take an elevator up 33 more stories to the SkyPod, the highest observation level.

3 CF Toronto Eaton Centre

People flock here *(see pp30–31)* for shopping and dining. The glass roof is modeled on a 19th-century Italian galleria.

4 Urban Forest

One look at Toronto from above and it's clear it's a green city – stately canopy trees line streets and snake along ravines.

1 City Hall

When opened in 1965, the building *(see p77)*, with its two curving towers **(above)**, was controversial in conservative Toronto. It has since become a much-loved icon of the city's modern architecture.

2 Fort York

Founded in 1793 and the site of the 1813 Battle of York, Fort York *(see p68)* has Canada's largest collection of buildings **(right)** from the War of 1812 era. Eight original structures still stand in the Fort, but many buildings were torn down during the 1950s.

5 Niagara Falls

If weather allows, you can see the mists rising above Niagara Falls *(see pp34–7)*, set 80 miles (130 km) to the southeast. The gentle curve of land along Lake Ontario reveals why the region is known as the Golden Horseshoe.

The distinctive CN Tower against the Toronto skyline

6 Roy Thomson Hall

The space-age design of this music hall *(see p52)*, located in the core of Toronto's theater district, features a distinctive glass canopy **(above)**.

7 Union Station

A relic from the days when passenger rail was the country's primary mode of transportation, this station *(see p45)* has lost none of its grandeur since it opened in 1927, still serving as an impressive gateway to the city.

8 Financial District

Soaring towers, such as those of the modernist Toronto-Dominion Centre *(see p68)*, signal the heart of Toronto's, and Canada's, financial district. The nation's major banks, insurance companies, and stockbrokers ply their trades, as wind-jostled workers hurry along the canyon-like streets.

9 Toronto Music Garden

The design of this garden *(see p67)*, inspired by the Baroque composer J. S. Bach, is best seen from above; the swirling paths and plantings do indeed seem musical.

10 Toronto Islands

This ribbon of islands *(see pp18–19)* shelters Toronto's harbor and provides a car-free retreat just a short ferry ride from downtown. The islands **(below)** have bike paths, picnic areas, beaches, and an amusement park *(see p50)*.

BUILDING FEATS

Considered one of the seven wonders of the modern world, the CN Tower is recognized as an unparalleled feat of modern engineering. It took 40 months to build the tower, with 1,537 workers working around the clock and pouring enough concrete to lay a sidewalk from Toronto to Kingston, 160 miles (260 km) away. A huge 10-ton Russian Sikorsky helicopter was used to lift the 44 pieces of the tower's 335-ft (102-m) antenna into place.

NEED TO KNOW

MAP J5 ■ 301 Front St W ■ 416 868 6937 ■ www.cntower.ca

Open 9am–10:30pm daily; closed Dec 25

Adm $38 adults, $34 senior citizens, $28 children aged 4–12 (add $15 for access to the SkyPod)

■ Reserve a table at the revolving 360 Restaurant *(416 362 5411)* to enjoy a slow-changing view. Elevation and access to the LookOut and Glass Floor levels are complementary following the purchase of a prix fixe by each guest.

■ Shop for unique souvenirs and genuine Canadiana at the Marketplace.

■ Test your nerve on the world's highest external walk on a building. CN Tower's EdgeWalk is a full-circle, hands-free walk on a 5-ft- (1.5-m-) wide ledge.

TOP 10 ⭐ Toronto Islands

The islands were formed when the rushing waters of the Don River separated a spit from the mainland during a storm in 1858. There are over a dozen islets and mid-sized islands in this archipelago, some of them connected by bridges, others accessible only by boat. A thriving community of creative characters calls Algonquin and Ward's islands home, while Centre Island is very popular for its amusement park. No cars are allowed here, adding to the tranquil charm. Along with walking, two great ways to get around are to hire a bike or rent a boat and paddle through the lagoon system.

CANADA'S CONEY ISLAND

Hanlan Point's heyday began in the 1880s as city dwellers flocked to its vaudeville theater, amusement park, dance hall, and hotels. Twenty years later, thousands of fans cheered on the baseball legend Babe Ruth as he hit his first professional home run, on September 5, 1914, at Hanlan Point's new stadium. By the end of 1937, however, the stadium and the fading resort had been torn down to make way for the Island Airport.

1 Ward's Island
Over 700 people live here in what began, in the 1880s, as a tiny tent settlement. Stroll along the pathways **(above)** and marvel at the creative ways in which the cottages have been adorned to the owners' tastes.

2 Ferry
Enjoy one of the best views to be had of the Toronto skyline aboard a ferry **(below)**, dating back to the 1950s, as it chugs across the lake to the Toronto Islands.

3 The Rectory
This restaurant also functions as Ward's Island social center. Main courses, soups, salads, and sandwiches are healthy and hearty, and the desserts are delicious.

7 Algonquin Island

The creativity of the islands' residents is most exuberantly expressed in their quirky, colorful gardens, which are in delightful bloom in the warmer months. The green thumb enthusiasts of Algonquin Island are often happy to share their tips with passersby.

10 Gibraltar Point Lighthouse

The oldest lighthouse **(below)** in the city has served as a shipping beacon since the early 19th century. The historic lime-stone landmark is rumored to be haunted by the ghost of its first keeper.

4 Far Enough Farm

Kids will love feeding and petting the lambs, goats, cows, pigs, and other farm animals **(above)** at this small petting zoo.

8 Boardwalk

The 1.5-mile (2.5-km) boardwalk runs from Ward's Island to Centre Island and is great for a lakeside stroll.

Toronto City Airport

Toronto Inner Harbour

Centre Island

Lake Ontario

Map of Toronto Islands

5 Bicycling

The best way to tour the islands is on wheels along the pedestrian-bicycle trails stretching the 4-mile (6-km) archipelago. Rent a one-person or tandem bike or quadracycle **(below)**.

6 Centreville Amusement Park

This small amusement park *(see p50)* on Centre Island has more than 30 rides, including swan boats and a colorful 1890s carousel.

9 Hanlan's Point

The point's two sandy beaches are pop-ular with sunbathers. In 1999, one of the beaches *(see p55)* reclaimed the clothing-optional status that it enjoyed when it first opened in 1894.

NEED TO KNOW

MAP B6–E6

Ferry: 416 397 2628; www.torontoisland. com/ferry.php

Bicycling: 416 203 0009; www.torontoisland bicyclerental.com

■ Fast-food spots on the islands are far apart and have seasonal hours.

■ Ferries depart from the terminal at the foot of Bay Street. Centre Island ferries operate summer and fall. Ward's Island and Hanlan's Point ferries run year-round.

■ The ferry ride ($8.19 adults, $5.37 senior citizens and students, $3.95 under 14s, free for under 2s) takes about 10 minutes. Bikes are permitted on board, except if it's busy. For booking, check website.

★ Art Gallery of Ontario

Founded in 1900, the wide-ranging Art Gallery of Ontario (AGO) has over 80,000 works. The outstanding pieces of Canadian art, in particular paintings by the Group of Seven, are a national treasure. Along with superb Henry Moore plasters, bronzes, and other works, the gallery exhibits significant masterpieces of European art, from paintings by Tintoretto and Frans Hals to Vincent van Gogh and Pablo Picasso. Other relevant acquisitions include an impressive collection of African and Australian indigenous art.

Group of Seven 1

Canadian landscapes epitomize these artists who strove, in the 1920s, to create a national artistic identity. The gallery's collection features works by MacDonald **(right)**, Jackson, Johnston, and Harris, among others.

2 Canadian Collection

These galleries **(above)** include First Nations and Inuit art, and Canadian luminaries such as Emily Carr, William Kurelek, and Alex Colville.

4 Photography

This collection has early work, with a large contribution from Czech photographer Josef Sudek, and photographs taken in the 1930s and 40s by the Klinsky Press Agency.

5 Inuit Art

This fine collection of works produced after World War II includes sculptures **(below)** and wall hangings made from indigenous materials.

3 Thomson Collection

This philanthropic cultural gift with 2,000 works adds remarkable depth to the AGO's collection, with emphasis on Tom Thomson and the Group of Seven, as well as 19th-century painters Cornelius Krieghoff and Paul Kane.

6 Contemporary

This collection covers American and European art since 1900 and Canadian art since 1985. Canadian artists represented here include Joanne Tod, Betty Goodwin, Elizabeth Magor, and Jeff Wall. Popular works such as *Venus Simultaneous* **(left)** by conceptual artist Michael Snow are featured here.

7 The AGO Kids' Gallery

This child-friendly gallery has themed exhibitions geared at young visitors. There's also an activity center, costumes, and a photo booth where kids can draw and pose for portraits of themselves.

8 Henry Moore

The world's largest public collection of works by British artist Henry Moore (1898–1986) encompasses bronze sculptures, plaster and bronze maquettes, drawings, and prints. His monumental *Large Two Forms* takes its place outdoors, with its surface now worn smooth by admirers' countless rubbings.

THE GRANGE

Set at the south end of the art gallery, the Grange was the first home of the AGO and was given National Historic Site status in 1970. The elegant Georgian mansion was constructed in 1817, when Toronto was just the small town of York in Upper Canada, and it reflects the conservative British tastes of the region at the time with its symmetrical five-bay facade and central pediment.

9 French Impressionists

Claude Monet, Camille Pissarro, and Pierre-Auguste Renoir **(above)** are just some of the 19th-century artists whose masterpieces grace this collection.

10 Prints and Drawings

The works in this collection range from the 15th to the 21st centuries and include important Italian, Dutch, German, French, and British pieces. *Adam and Eve* (1504) by German artist Albrecht Dürer is a highlight. Works by Canadians also feature strongly.

NEED TO KNOW

MAP J3 ■ 317 Dundas St W ■ 1 877 225 4246 ■ www.ago.net

Open 10:30am–5:30pm Tue, Thu, Sat & Sun (until 9pm Wed & Fri)

Adm $19.50 adults aged 26 and above, $16 senior citizens, $49 family ticket, free 6–9pm Wednesday, $35 annual membership with unlimited visits

■ The Lower Level café offers a family-friendly lunch menu, while the upmarket AGO Bistro offers a global menu.

■ Browse the Gallery Shop for specialty gifts, reproductions from the gallery's collection, books, and handcrafted jewelry.

■ Join one of the free tours for extra insight into the collections and exhibits. Call the information line for details.

Casa Loma

This Edwardian-style castle, completed in 1914 for a staggering $3.5 million, looms on a hill, overlooking downtown. It was designed by the famed Toronto architect E. J. Lennox, who was responsible for many of the city's historic buildings. Casa Loma – Spanish for "house on the hill" – was the estate of prominent financier and industrialist Sir Henry Pellatt, who was forced by financial ruin to abandon his 98-room dream home less than 10 years after it was built.

1 Towers

Stunning views reward those not afraid of heights. Climb up to the top and survey the property from its highest perch. The east tower **(below)** is based on Scottish castle design, while the west tower, of Norman design, offers a breathtaking view of the city.

NEED TO KNOW

MAP C2 ▪ 1 Austin Terrace ▪ 416 923 1171 ▪ www.casaloma.org

Open 9:30am–5pm daily (last admittance 4pm); closed Jan 1 & Dec 25

Adm $25 adults, $20 senior citizens and youth aged 14–17, $15 children aged 4–13

▪ Grab a bite at the Liberty Café, open daily.

▪ Wander the castle on your own with a self-guided audio tour, available at no charge in eight languages.

▪ The colorful estate gardens are open from May through October, weather permitting.

2 Sir Henry's Bathroom

This room is heavy on hedonistic comfort, with the shower designed to completely surround the body with sprays of water from above and from the sides, and six large taps controlling three levels of pipes. The walls are made of Carrara marble.

3 Sir Henry's Study

The wood panels by the fireplace conceal two secret passages. The one to the right gave Sir Henry quick access to the wine cellar and his huge wine collection. The one to the left emerged on the second floor, near his bedroom suite.

4 Great Hall

The grand entrance hall **(below)**, with its 60-ft- (18-m-) high ceiling, sets the castle's tone of splendor. Gargoyles grin down on visitors from the pillars. Audio guide tapes are available here.

Previous pages The magnificent facade of Casa Loma

7 Conservatory

A magnificent set of bronze-and-glass doors costing $10,000, are reproductions of a set made for an Italian villa. The intricate stained-glass ceiling dome **(left)**, from Italy, was originally backlit by 600 light bulbs, so that it glowed at night.

FIRST IN LUXURY

As the founder of the Toronto Electric Light Company, Sir Henry Pellatt brought electric power to the city, so it is not surprising that his home featured a range of innovations that enhanced comfort on a scale never before seen in a Canadian home. These included an electric lighting system controlled from a panel in Sir Henry's bedroom, a central vacuuming system, forced-air heating, and the city's first electric elevator in a private home.

9 Round Room

With doors and windows custom-bowed to align with the curved walls, this lovely room is furnished with period pieces. Sir Pellatt's suite of carved Louis XV chairs and folding screen are upholstered in rare French tapestry.

5 Oak Room

It took artisans 3 full years to carve the magnificent French oak paneling in this drawing room **(above)**. The plaster ceiling moldings conceal indirect lighting. It was the first time such lighting was used in a Canadian home.

6 Tunnel

Beneath the floors, a tunnel connects the castle to the carriage house and stables, where horses were kept. An exhibit tells the story of the city's dark days, including the Plague, the Prohibition, and the Depression.

8 Library

Stripes of light and dark wood in the herringbone oak floor create an optical illusion of different shadings from each end of the room. The elaborate plaster ceiling features portrait busts and the family's coats of arms.

10 Gardens

Lavish gardens **(above)**, punctuated by sculptures and fountains, grace the estate with blooms in season. Eight themed areas range from formal rose beds to woodland with luscious spring wild flowers.

Distillery Historic District

Walking the pedestrian-only cobblestone streets past the beautifully preserved Victorian industrial architecture, you'll feel as if you've stumbled into another century. The buildings of this 13-acre (5-ha) site were, until 1990, part of Gooderham and Worts, once the world's largest distillery; the distillery evolved from a grist mill founded here in 1832. The 150-year-old district has been infused with new life and is a vibrant area of cafés, restaurants, galleries, art studios, performance venues, and specialty shops.

1 Boiler House Complex
In the 1860s, the boiler house heated the entire distillery. Other buildings in the complex housed a carpentry shop, a blacksmith, and a canteen. They have now been converted into restaurants and a bakery.

2 Corkin Gallery
Fronted with huge windows to let in natural light and diminish the fire hazard of producing alcohol under gas lighting, this 1873 building is the perfect setting for the art and photography exhibitions **(above)** within.

3 Balzac's Coffee
The pumps in this building were connected to the underground reservoir, in case of fire; others were used for alcohol. It is now home to Balzac's Coffee **(above)**; beans are roasted Mondays and Fridays.

4 Bergo Designs
Though expensive, this design shop has some of the district's most interesting items and is worth a browse.

NEED TO KNOW

MAP E5 ■ 55 Mill St (Take the 504 King streetcar or Parliament Street bus 65 from Castle Frank to King and Parliament, then walk south on Parliament) ■ www.thedistillerydistrict.com

■ Many of the district's restaurants and cafés have large patios set amongst the historic buildings. With no traffic or exhaust fumes, the Distillery District is a perfect place to dine on a summer evening.

■ Join a guided tour ($19) or a Segway tour ($39 for 30 minutes; $69 for an hour) to get the most out of your visit. Check website www.segwayofontario.com or call 416 642 0008.

■ The district hosts many festivals and events throughout the summer and a popular Christmas Market in December.

6 Young Centre for the Performing Arts

Housed in Tank House No. 9 and No. 10 **(left)**, where whiskey was stored while it aged, this is the main performance space of Soulpepper, the city's largest theater company *(see p53)*.

9 Artscape Distillery Studios

The majority of arts organizations and artists in the distillery complex have their offices, workshops, and studios in these brick-fronted buildings where liquor was once stored.

Map of Distillery Historic District

7 Arta Gallery

Located just off Parliament Street, and with the same old-world charm as the district itself, this gallery occupies a building that once housed a huge tank of molasses for rum.

8 Mill Street Brewery

While many of the distillery buildings still smell faintly of the grain and alcohol once stored within, this 1879 building renews its scent of malt and hops daily, from the Mill Street Brewery. Traditional handcrafted beers include an organic lager and a robust coffee porter. While sipping samples at The Beer Hall, explore the display of vintage distilling equipment.

10 Thompson Landry Gallery

This gallery, showcasing Quebec artists, is set in a huge limestone structure, the oldest in the complex. Its exterior still retains features, such as a winch, from the days when the lakeshore – and ships – came right up to the building.

5 Caffe Furbo

This café **(below)** in the heart of the district occupies a building once used for canning industrial-grade alcohol. It now offers both delicious food and art to enjoy with it.

FILMING AT THE DISTILLERY

When the Gooderham and Worts Distillery ceased operations in 1990, the entire site, with its wonderfully evocative atmosphere, began a new life as the largest film set outside Hollywood. Hundreds of film shoots took place here during the 1990s, including *Chicago*, *The Hurricane*, and *X-Men*, along with popular television series such as *La Femme Nikita* and *Alfred Hitchcock Presents*, making this Canada's busiest filming location.

TOP 10 ⭐ Ripley's Aquarium of Canada

Crouched at the base of the CN Tower, this hulking wave-like structure opened in 2013. Inside, over 16,000 marine animals glide and float within stunningly displayed fresh- and saltwater tanks, some several stories deep, others floating overhead. The Discovery Centre has play equipment for when the kids start to feel fished-out.

Whether you're surrounded on all sides by saw-tooth fish or getting to know a zebra shark from a perspex bubble, it's great fun.

1 Sea Dragons, The Gallery

At first glance, you may only notice elaborate seaweed. Look again. Otherworldly weedy and leafy sea dragons (above) float gracefully by.

2 Piranhas

These deceptively peaceful, glittering predators have their own tank.

3 Rainbow Reef

A wonderful sea of color awaits at this Indo-Pacific reef (above) where vibrant coral compete with an array of neon species of fish.

4 Discovery Centre

Pet a horseshoe crab at the touch pool and surround yourself with clown fish (above) in the peek-a-boo tanks. A water table with locks, dams, and fish-runs demonstrates the complexity of shipping going through the Great Lakes.

Floor Plan of Ripley's Aquarium of Canada

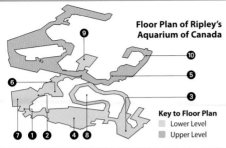

Key to Floor Plan
- Lower Level
- Upper Level

AQUARIUM GUIDE

Start on the Upper Level with Canadian Waters. A ramp winds around the Pacific Kelp down to the Dangerous Lagoon and then on to the Discovery Centre. Continue on to Perfect Predators and through Planet Jellies to the ramp back up to the Upper Level past the filtration systems of the Life Support System. Exit via the gift shop.

9 Planet Jellies
The stars of the gallery, the Pacific Sea Nettle jellyfish (above) put on a stunning display of contrasting colors.

5 Great Lakes, Canadian Waters
Bass, pike, carp, trout, catfish, and the comical longnose gar – visitors may be surprised to see just how large the fish from the Great Lakes Basin can grow.

6 Ray Bay
Graceful Southern, Cownose, and Roughtail rays seem to fly through the waters. The floor-to-ceiling tank gives the rays plenty of room to swoop and dive, skimming right past the faces of dazzled observers.

7 The Gallery
Piranhas, pipefish, seahorses and other species demonstrate their remarkable camouflage skills in this huge tank populated with live coral.

8 Dangerous Lagoon
A 315-ft (96-m) underwater tunnel takes visitors through the aquarium's largest tank where sharks (below) steal the show.

10 Pacific Kelp, Canadian Waters
Strands of kelp provide a roomy home for over 25 species that swim off Canada's West Coast.

TOP 10 ⭐ CF Toronto Eaton Centre

This upscale mall is named for Canadian retail legend Timothy Eaton, whose department store, Eaton's, was a national institution until 1999, when the company declared bankruptcy. Big, busy, and boisterous, this quintessential downtown mall was opened in 1977 and heralded as the anchor that would transform down-at-heel Yonge and Dundas streets into an upscale destination. The complex now houses some 250 stores, restaurants, and cafés, including Canada's first Saks Fifth Avenue and Toronto's first Nordstrom.

1 Flight Stop
Suspended in the central atrium is this sculpted gaggle of geese by Toronto artist Michael Snow, so life-like that you almost expect to hear the geese honk.

2 The Labyrinth
This circuitous grass path is modeled on the 13th-century labyrinth at Chartres Cathedral in France.

3 Fountain
A focal point of the mall, this waterburst fountain **(below)** lulls visitors with soothing sounds of falling water, then astonishes as water shoots 100 ft (30 m) into the air. Surrounded by benches, the fountain is a good spot for a break.

5 Galleria
Natural light pours through the soaring glass roof into the arcade **(above)**, designed by Eb Zeidler and modeled on the 19th-century Galleria Vittorio Emanuele in Milan. Nordstrom is located at the north end, while Hudson's Bay and Saks Fifth Avenue anchor the south end.

4 Scadding House
Built in 1857 for the Church of the Holy Trinity's first rector, this Georgian-Gothic house was moved here to make way for the mall. The church and house may be Yonge Street's oldest building complex. The current rector lives in the house.

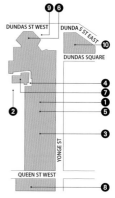

Map of CF Toronto Eaton Centre

7 Church of the Holy Trinity

This Anglican church **(left)** dating to 1847 is an oasis of calm amid the commercial bustle. Admire the turreted entranceway and then step inside to see the stained-glass windows.

8 Hudson's Bay

Canada's largest department store chain, Hudson's Bay sells a wide selection of merchandise but might be best known for its point blankets, first used to barter for beaver pelts with the Cree of the First Nations. Its trading posts, based in the vast north of what is now Canada, were influential centers of commerce.

9 Bronze Plaque

This historic plaque commemorates Yonge Street, ranked the longest street in the world by the Guinness Book of World Records. Yonge Street divides East and West Toronto and is the site of the city's first subway line.

6 PATH

From the CF Toronto Eaton Centre you can access the 18-mile (30-km) or so underground walkway PATH. Linking several attractions, PATH winds through stores and food courts.

10 Yonge-Dundas Square

Toronto's once-tawdry intersection is now a public square **(below)** embellished with 22 fountains. Events take place here, especially during the summer.

HUDSON'S BAY COMPANY (HBC)

The HBC controlled the continent's lucrative fur trade for 200 years. It was so powerful that it made laws and even waged war with indigenous tribes. After years of fierce English-French battles over its posts, it lost its monopoly, and, in 1870, it sold its land to the Government of Canada. Moving to retail, the HBC opened its first store in 1881, but kept a hand in the fur trade until 1991, when its last fur salon closed.

NEED TO KNOW

MAP L3 ■ 220 Yonge St (alternative entrances along Yonge St between Dundas and Queen, and at Queen St west of Yonge St) ■ 416 598 8560 ■ www.toronto eatoncentre.com

Open 10am–9:30pm Mon–Fri, 9:30am–9:30pm Sat & 10am–7pm Sun; closed Dec 25

■ The Urban Eatery in the basement at the north end of the mall has a range of food counters. Trinity Square Café, in the Church of the Holy Trinity, is open weekdays for lunch.

■ Take a ride up the Eaton Center's glass elevators, located near the central fountain, for a wonderful view of the galleria from above.

■ Navigate PATH using the color-coded signs: the red P steers you south; the orange A west, the blue T north; and the yellow H east.

★ Hockey Hall of Fame

This shrine to Canada's favorite sport is housed in part of a beautiful former bank building dating to 1885, and it contains the most comprehensive collection of hockey memorabilia in the world, among which is the original Stanley Cup trophy. Interactive exhibits run the gamut from multimedia trivia kiosks that test your hockey knowledge to a virtual-reality puck-shooting game that allows visitors to go one-on-one against life-size, animated versions of top players.

1 Stanley Cup
One of the world's best-known trophies, the original Stanley Cup is on display here, as is the current one. Named for the country's sixth Governor General, it was first presented in 1893.

2 Montreal Canadiens Locker Room
The only thing missing from this re-created locker room **(below)** from the old Montreal Forum is the players.

3 Goalie Mask Exhibit
This fun display includes several strange examples of face protection **(left)** that have been personalized by goalies over the years.

4 Game Time Zone
On a faux ice rink, with arena boards and multimedia scoreboard, shoot a puck at a life-sized video-projection goalie, or be the goalie facing simulated shots by greats Sidney Crosby and Alexander Ovechkin.

5 Great Hall
Players and icons of hockey are celebrated in this 45-ft- (14-m-) high former banking hall **(above)**. Giants of the game appear on the Honoured Members Wall, and all major NHL trophies are on display.

NEED TO KNOW

MAP L5 ■ 30 Yonge St (enter through Brookfield Pl concourse) ■ 416 360 7765 ■ www.hhof.com

Open daily (hours vary seasonally); closed Jan 1, Dec 25 and induction day

Adm $20 adults, $16 senior citizens, $14 children, free for under 4s

■ Many of the eateries in Brookfield Place *(see p44)* have seating options in the spectacular glass-canopied galleria. A food court on the lower level provides light snacks for those on the go.

■ If your energy flags, take a seat in one of the Hall of Fame's two theater venues to watch a retrospective video or a presentation.

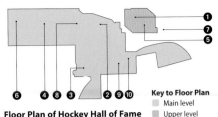

Floor Plan of Hockey Hall of Fame

Key to Floor Plan
- Main level
- Upper level

8 Movie Theaters
The Hall of Fame's two theaters screen games and highlights. You can also enjoy hockey's first 3D movie, Stanley's Game Seven.

6 Broadcast Zone
With state-of-the-art technology, visitors can experience the TV broadcast world from different angles, both on and off the camera, including calling the play-by-play or testing sports anchor skills in front of a camera.

7 Our Game
Exuberant young players leap over the boards for a hockey game in this larger-than-life bronze sculpture **(below)** by Ontario artist Edie Parker. Located just outside the museum at Yonge and Front streets, it is a popular backdrop for photographs.

The Golden Goal

9 Golden Goal Display
The Golden Goal exhibit **(above)** features Sidney Crosby's podium, "Golden Net," stick, puck, and gloves from the 2010 Winter Olympics.

10 Spirit of Hockey Shop
The museum's exit takes visitors through this shop. Hockey-themed merchandise includes a wide selection of team jerseys, sticks, and other items printed with logos.

🔟 ⭐ Niagara Falls

One of the world's most famous natural attractions, Niagara Falls is a dazzling spectacle of great arcs of hissing, frothing water crashing over cliffs 20 stories high. Drifting spray adds to the excitement of being near the edge of a stomach-churning drop. The 188-ft- (57-m-) high Canadian Horseshoe Falls is the mightiest of the three cataracts that make up the falls, while across the Niagara River lie the American Falls and the smaller Bridal Veil Falls. When visiting, take time to stop at some of the other sights in the region, including its renowned vineyards, historic museums, and the small, charming town of Niagara-on-the-Lake.

1 Voyage to the Falls

Experience the mighty falls from below on a Hornblower Niagara Cruise. The 20-minute voyage takes you to the Great Gorge, American Falls, Bridal Veil Falls, and into the spray of Horseshoe Falls.

2 American Falls

New York State, on the US side of the inter-national border, lays claim to this cataract. Its 950-ft- (290-m-) wide crest sees only a fraction of the volume of water that is carried over by the Horseshoe Falls.

3 Journey Behind the Falls

Rock tunnels, behind the Horseshoe Falls, lead you past a wall of water so thick it blocks out daylight. The vantage point **(below)**, beneath the gorge's rim, is inspiring. Rain ponchos are provided.

Map of Niagara Falls

4 The Old Scow

Shipwrecked in 1918, this barge is now stranded on rocks. The two-man crew survived but had to wait 29 hours near the brink of the falls before being rescued.

8 Whirlpool Rapids

A sharp turn in the river just downstream of the falls creates a raging whirlpool. Look down on the rapids from a cable-car **(left)** traversing this lethal stretch of water.

5 Horseshoe Falls

This 2,200-ft- (670-m-) wide cataract is formed as 90 per cent of the water of the Niagara River, the outlet from Lake Erie to Lake Ontario, roars over a semicircular cliff **(below)** of the Niagara Escarpment.

FORCEFUL FLOW

The forces of erosion that created the falls are today responsible for wearing them away. Before hydroelectric stations were built on the Niagara River, the rock face eroded by up to 6 ft (1.8 m) a year. It is now just 1 ft (30 cm) annually. Almost a fifth of the Earth's freshwater flows over the falls – so much that it is thought that it would take only an hour to fill a ditch between Canada's east and west coasts.

6 Butterfly Conservatory

The conservatory is a huge heated dome with thousands of colorful creatures **(below)** flitting freely about – and sometimes landing on delighted visitors.

9 Table Rock

Stand mere feet from Horseshoe Falls, only a rail between you and a torrent of water. The lookout point was so named because it extended over the gorge like a table leaf. Deemed unstable in 1935, the ledge was blasted off.

10 Niagara Parks Botanical Gardens

These beautiful gardens **(above)**, close to the falls, include a splendid rose display with more than 2,000 varieties.

7 White Water Walk

Descend from the top of the chasm by elevator to a tunnel leading to a riverside boardwalk. The whirlpools and rapids here are among the most spectacular, and treacherous, in the world.

NEED TO KNOW

MAP Q3

Visitor Info: 5400 Robinson St; 905 356 6061 & 1 800 563 2557; discount passes available online; www. niagarafallstourism.com

Voyage to the Falls: $25.95 adults, $15.95 children, free for under 4s; www. niagaracruises.com

■ Windows by Jamie Kennedy *(www.windows byjamiekennedy.com)* offers fine dining with great views of the falls.

■ The Adventure Pass includes a Hornblower Cruise, Journey Behind the Falls, White Water Walk, Niagara's Fury, and WEGO shuttle bus rides *(www.niagaraparks.com)*.

Things to Do Around Niagara Falls

(1) Fallsview Casino Resort
6380 Fallsview Blvd, Niagara Falls ■ 1 888 325 5788 ■ Open daily
Try your luck at the largest gaming resort in Canada. The Fallsview Casino Resort hosts 3,000 slot machines, 130 gaming tables, spa, hotel, shops, and restaurants.

All the fun of the fair at Clifton Hill

(2) Clifton Hill
Niagara Falls
This is the center of Niagara Falls' entertainment, home to museums, mini-golf, and Midway, with hotels and restaurants for all budgets.

(3) Helicopter Tours
Niagara Helicopters (10 mins): 1 800 281 8034 ■ National Helicopters (20 mins): 1 800 491 3117 ■ adm
Experience the exhilaration of swooping over the falls.

(4) IMAX Theatre Niagara Falls
6170 Fallsview Blvd, Niagara Falls ■ 866 405 4629 ■ Adm
■ www.imaxniagara.com
Niagara: Miracles, Myths and Magic chronicles the history of the falls. Projected onto a giant screen, the movie makes you feel like you're right in the midst of things. Original stunt barrels are displayed in the theater's Daredevil Gallery.

(5) Welland Canal
Lock 3 Viewing Complex & Museum: Government Rd, St. Catharines ■ 1 800 305 5134 ■ Open 9am–5pm daily
Linking Lake Ontario and Lake Erie, this eight-lock, 27-mile (43-km) canal opened in 1829, allowing vessels to traverse the Niagara Escarpment – and the 328-ft (100-m) difference in height between the lakes. The canalside trail from Thorold to St. Catharines is great for ship-gazing.

(6) Queenston Heights Park
Niagara River Pkwy, Niagara Falls
A monument pays tribute to General Brock, a leader of the British forces killed in battle here during the War of 1812, when the US invaded Upper Canada *(see p68)*. With great views of Niagara River, the park is an excellent spot for a picnic.

(7) Old Fort Erie
350 Lakeshore Rd, Ft Erie ■ 905 871 0540 ■ Open mid-May– Oct: 10am–5pm daily ■ Adm
This reconstructed fort, which was a supply base for British troops in the 1700s, was also the site of many battles with US forces throughout the 1800s.

(8) Skylon Tower
5200 Robinson St ■ 905 356 2651 ■ Open summer: 8am–midnight daily; winter: 9am–midnight ■ Adm
A viewing deck affording vistas of as far as 80 miles (130 km). This tower rises 775 ft (236 m) above the falls. The popular revolving restaurant offers fine dining.

Revolving dining, Skylon Tower

Re-enactment at Fort George

the War of 1812 between Britain and the US *(see p68)*. It has been restored to the period, with replica buildings and costumed staff playing host.

(9) Fort George
51 Queen's Parade, Niagara-on-the-Lake ▪ 905 468 6614 ▪ Open May–Aug: 10am–5pm daily; Sep–Apr: noon–4pm Sat & Sun ▪ Adm

This historic British fort, built in 1796, was a key defense post during

(10) Great Wolf Lodge
3950 Victoria Ave, Niagara Falls ▪ 905 354 4888 ▪ www.greatwolf.com

Splash the day away at this massive family-friendly waterpark complex. Thrilling slides for all ages, animatronic animals, and "family dance party" sessions complete the Great Wolf experience. A bowling alley and arcade games add to the fun.

DAREDEVIL FEATS

For some 200 years, daredevils have risked their lives at Niagara Falls. Many have had close calls; about 20 have lost their lives. The first daredevil, Sam Patch, dove headfirst from an 85-ft- (26-m-) high platform into the churning Niagara River in 1829 and survived. Ten days later he did it again, from a height of 130 ft (40 m). The Great Blondin crossed the gorge on a tightrope nine times in 1859. When Blondin returned in 1860 for more stunts, such as pushing a wheelbarrow across the rope, he was challenged by a young upstart, the Great Farini, who crossed carrying a washing machine. Farini became increasingly daring, doing headstands and hanging by his toes. He survived them all and died at the age of 91. The first woman funambulist, Maria Spelterini, crossed blindfolded, in 1876. The first woman to survive going over the falls in a barrel was Annie Taylor, in 1901.

TOP 10 NIAGARA DAREDEVILS

1 Jean Francois Gravelot, aka The Great Blondin, tightrope crossing, 1859

2 Guillermo Antonio Farini, aka The Great Farini, stilt tightrope crossing, 1864

3 Henry Bellini, tightrope crossing and leap into river, 1873

4 Maria Spelterini, first woman to cross on a tightrope, 1876

5 Carlisle Graham, first man over the falls in a barrel, 1886

6 Clifford Calverly, fastest tightrope crossing, 1887

7 James Hardy, youngest tightrope crosser (21), 1896

8 Annie Edson Taylor, first woman over the falls in a barrel, 1901

9 Lincoln Beachy, first airplane stunt at the falls, 1911

10 Nik Wallenda, tightrope crossing, 2012

Blondin couldn't get enough of Niagara Falls, crossing on a tightrope many times.

The Top 10
of Everything

The Michael Lee-Chin Crystal extension
at the Royal Ontario Museum

🔟 Moments in History

Illustration of explorer Étienne Brûlé

1 Europeans Arrive

In the 17th century, Europeans made their way to the region now known as Toronto. The first French explorer to reach the shores of Lake Ontario was Étienne Brûlé. He spent many years among the Huron-Wendat people learning their language and mapping the land. By 1720, the French established trading posts such as Fort Rouillé for trade with the indigenous population.

2 Fort York Built

The origins of the city can be traced back to Fort York (see p16), a colonial stockade (see p68) built in 1793 to maintain a naval presence on Lake Ontario due to a war threat with the United States in the years following the American Revolution (1765–1783). The fort served as the city's primary harbor defence between the 1790s and 1880s, housing a military garrison until the 1930s.

3 Parliament of York Founded

The first parliament buildings in York (present day Toronto) served as the meeting place of the Legislative Assembly of Upper Canada (present day Ontario) from 1797 to 1813. Located near the intersection of today's Parliament and Front streets, these were the first two buildings, in the town of York, to be built of brick. Besides the House of Commons and the Senate, they also housed the courts of justice and held church services for the city congregation.

4 Battle of York

During the War of 1812 (see p68), a fleet of American troops made its way to York since it was considered to be an easier target than the main British base at Kingston. American forces occupied the town for 11 days and burned public property, including the parliament buildings, and seized valuable military supplies before abandoning the town. Later, it was reclaimed by the British.

5 University of Toronto Established

Founded by the royal charter in 1827 as King's College, the University of Toronto (see p78) was secularized and renamed in 1849. The first degree was awarded in 1850. In the 20th century, the university rapidly diversified by introducing new faculties, such as forestry, nursing, and social work.

6 York named Toronto

The origin of the name is debated as phonetic echoes of "Toronto" have been found in the languages of indigenous groups that inhabited the region at different points in time. The settlement of York was named by Lieutenant Governor John Graves Simcoe who preferred the use of English names over indigenous ones. By the 1830s, York's regional importance and the population expanded. The incorporation of York by the Legislative Council as the City of Toronto on March 6, 1834 also allowed the disassociation from the derogatory "dirty little York" – a common nickname used by the residents.

7 Irish Migrate to Toronto

The Great Famine of the late 1840s, a period of starvation and disease caused by the total failure of the potato crop, led to the mass emigration of the Irish to the rapidly expanding city of Toronto. By 1871, the Irish were the largest ethnic group in most Canadian cities.

8 Old City Hall Built

Upon its completion in 1899, the Old City Hall (see p45) was the largest building in the city. It was designed by famous architect E. J. Lennox (see p24), who was also referred to as the "builder of Toronto." In the 20th century, the hall (see p78) was deemed insufficient to meet the demands of an expanding city and the New City Hall (see p77) was built to replace it.

Grand facade of the Old City Hall

9 Megacity Toronto

Five sprawling municipalities of Etobicoke, Scarborough, North York, East York, and York were amalgamated into the metropolitan Toronto's larger municipal umbrella in 1998. This new unified city was colloquially referred to as the "Megacity."

10 Invictus Games hosted by Toronto

Founded in 2014 by Prince Harry, the Duke of Sussex, the Invictus Games were hosted by Toronto in 2017. A multi-sport event for wounded and injured armed forces' members and veterans, the games also helped spread awareness about the many challenges faced by army veterans.

TOP 10 FAMOUS TORONTONIANS

Popular author, Margaret Atwood

1 J. J. R. Macleod (1876–1935) and Frederick Banting (1891–1941)
Macleod and Banting were awarded the Nobel Prize in Physiology or Medicine in 1923 for their discovery of insulin.

2 Frank Gehry (b. 1929)
One of the foremost contemporary architects, Gehry is known for his postmodern designs, including the Dundas Street facade of the AGO (see pp20–21).

3 Margaret Atwood (b. 1939)
A Man Booker Prize-winner, Atwood has penned several poems and novels, including The Handmaid's Tale.

4 Dave Keon (b. 1940)
Inducted into the Hockey Hall of Fame (see pp32–3), Keon won four Stanley Cups for the Toronto Maple Leafs.

5 Michael Ondaatje (b. 1943)
Sri Lankan-born Canadian poet and author, Ondaatje has won many prestigious awards, including the Booker Prize.

6 Joni Mitchell (b. 1943)
Legendary folk singer who got her start performing in bars in Yorkville.

7 Jim Carrey (b. 1962)
A stand-up comedian popular in the late 1970s Toronto comedy scene, Jim Carrey also acted in movies such as Bruce Almighty.

8 Keanu Reeves (b. 1964)
This Hollywood actor is known for The Matrix and the John Wick film franchise.

9 Samantha Bee (b. 1969)
First woman to host a late-night show, Bee was a correspondent on The Daily Show – a satirical TV news program.

10 Drake (b. 1986)
Grammy award-winning Drakes' albums have sold millions of copies.

Museums and Galleries

1 Royal Ontario Museum

Canada's foremost museum (see pp12–15) offers an excellent balance of art, archeology, science, and nature, with over six million artifacts in its collections.

2 Gardiner Museum of Ceramic Art

Founded in 1984 by Canadian collectors George and Helen Gardiner, the museum (see p78) showcases their collection of pre-Columbian American pottery and European porcelain. Later additions include Asian ceramics and contemporary art.

Figure, Gardiner Museum of Ceramic Art

3 McMichael Canadian Art Collection

The outstanding Group of Seven collection features at this gallery (see p96). The Group endeavored, in the early 20th century, to express a national identity through their paintings of the Canadian wilderness.

4 Power Plant Contemporary Art Gallery

Known for its boundary-pushing contemporary Canadian and international art, this edgy, non-collecting gallery (see p70) features rotating shows of consistently high quality. If the art sometimes mystifies visitors, at least the building is instantly recognizable – a brick smokestack tops the 1920s converted power station.

5 Art Gallery of Ontario

Reflecting some 600 years of human creative endeavor, this gallery's permanent collection (see pp20–21) contains more than 80,000 works in all media. The Canadian collection is particularly impressive.

6 Textile Museum of Canada

MAP K3 ▪ 55 Centre Ave ▪ 416 599 5321 ▪ Open 11am–5pm daily (until 8pm Wed) ▪ Adm ▪ www.textilemuseum.ca

A permanent collection of over 10,000 fabrics, quilts, ceremonial cloths, and carpets from around the world are housed in this small but excellent museum. Temporary contemporary exhibits round out the historical artifacts.

7 Bata Shoe Museum

This unusual building (see p76), resembling a shoebox, houses more than 13,000 artifacts, covering 4,500 years of footwear history. Artifacts represent an unparalleled range, from Ancient Egyptian funerary shoes (1500 BC) to 19th-century Nigerian camel-riding boots to Elvis Presley's patent blue loafers.

8 Ontario Science Centre

The hundreds of interactive exhibits here (see p95) make science fascinating and fun. Youthful visitors can touch a tornado, navigate their way in a rocket chair, explore the hair-raising effects of electricity, send paper whooshing up a wind tunnel, and construct ramps and loops for balls to whiz around on.

9 Aga Khan Museum

This architecturally stunning museum *(see p96)* showcases the artistic and scientific heritage of Muslim civilizations from the Iberian Peninsula to China. Artifacts, dating from the 8th through the 21st centuries, include manuscripts, paintings, and ceramics. The museum auditorium hosts a varied cultural program through the year, and the public gardens are a tranquil spot for a break.

Auditorium, Aga Khan Museum

10 Toronto Dominion Gallery of Inuit Art

Most of the 200 pieces in this gallery *(see p70)* specializing in postwar Inuit sculpture are carved soapstone, each evocative of the landscape, culture, and legends of the indigenous people of Canada's harsh Arctic region. The gallery's design echoes that of the TD Bank Tower, by modernist architect Mies van der Rohe.

The futuristic Ontario Science Centre

TOP 10 SMALL MUSEUMS

Visitors at Campbell House

1 Campbell House
This is the oldest remaining building *(see p77)* dating from 1822 in the city.

2 Mackenzie House
The home *(see p87)* of Toronto's first mayor, William Lyon Mackenzie.

3 Toronto's First Post Office
A historic museum and also a working post office *(see p89)*.

4 TIFF Bell Lightbox
MAP J4 ▪ 350 King St W ▪ 416 599 8433 ▪ Adm ▪ www.tiff.net
Film-focused exhibitions at the HQ of the Toronto International Film Festival.

5 MOCA
158 Sterling Road ▪ 416 395 0067 ▪ Adm ▪ museumof contemporaryart.ca
Innovative works by emerging artists.

6 Redpath Sugar Museum
MAP M6 ▪ 95 Queens Quay E ▪ 416 933 8341 ▪ www.redpathsugar.com
Next door to a refinery, this museum tells the history of sugar production.

7 St. Lawrence Market Gallery
This second-floor gallery *(see p90)* has exhibits on art, culture, and history.

8 University of Toronto Art Centre
MAP J1 ▪ 15 King's College Circle ▪ www.artmuseum.utoronto.ca
The impressive art collection behind University College is housed here.

9 Design Exchange
Canadian design is showcased in the Art Deco building *(see p70)* that was once the Toronto Stock Exchange.

10 Stratford Perth Museum
This museum *(see p101)* showcases an eclectic mix of exhibits and collections, including artifacts ranging from the 20th century to the contemporary times.

⊞10 Architectural Highlights

University College, the founding college of the University of Toronto

1 University of Toronto
Founded in 1827 as King's College, this institute *(see p78)* has many stately, refined buildings, such as the Romanesque Revival-style University College.

2 Brookfield Place
MAP L5 ■ 181 Bay St

Spanish architect Santiago Calatrava designed the striking atrium of this 1990 office complex. Its steel-and-glass canopy creates enchanting patterns of light and shadow.

Glass arcade of the Brookfield Place

3 CN Tower
Defining the skyline, Toronto's most recognizable architectural icon *(see p16–17)* is also the tallest building in the Western Hemisphere.

4 Toronto-Dominion Centre
Two austere, perfectly proportioned towers and a single-story pavilion of glass and black metal are Toronto's only design by International Style architect Ludwig Mies van der Rohe (1886–1969). Completed in 1971, the complex *(see p68)* spurred the skyscraper boom that gave birth to the city's financial district. Four more towers were later added.

5 Royal Bank Plaza
MAP K4 ■ 200 Bay St

The 14,000 mirrored windows of the two towers (1977) are insulated with 24-karat gold. There is $70 worth of gold on each window, totalling some $1 million – money saved on heating.

6 The L Tower
MAP L5 ■ 22 The Esplanade

Set beside the Meridian Hall *(see p52)*, this 58-story skyscraper of condos was designed by Daniel Libeskind. Its towering curve makes it the most elegant high-rise in the city.

7 Old City Hall

Now serving as a courthouse, this Richardsonian Romanesque building (see p78), completed in 1899, was designed by the architect responsible for many of Toronto's grandest historic buildings, E. J. Lennox. For the best view of its clock tower, look north up Bay Street.

8 Sharpe Centre for Design

MAP J3 ▪ 100 McCaul St

Propped up on 100-ft (30-m) stilts, this addition to the Ontario College of Art and Design is playful and audacious. The two-story "tabletop" style building connects to the main building via a sloping tunnel.

9 Union Station

MAP K5 ▪ 65 Front St W

The Great Hall of this 1920s monumental stone railroad station (see p17) has vaulted ceiling that is 88 ft (27 m) high.

10 City Hall

Causing a significant stir in 1960s Toronto, the design of New City Hall (see p77) is unique, daring, and bold. Finnish architect Viljo Revell's two curving towers seem to embrace the central domed structure between them. A sweeping public plaza out front, Nathan Phillips Square, is the symbolic heart of the city.

The distinctive towers of City Hall

TOP 10 PUBLIC ART SITES

King Street exhibit, *The Pasture*

1 The Pasture
MAP L4 ▪ 77 King St W
Joe Fafard's seven bronze, life-size cows are in gentle repose.

2 Three Way Piece No. 2
MAP K3 ▪ Nathan Phillips Sq
Also known as *The Archer*, this Henry Moore bronze, controversial when installed in 1966, is now a local favorite.

3 Immigrant Family
MAP L5 ▪ 18 Yonge St
This tomato-shaped family by sculptor Tom Otterness is thought-provoking.

4 Toronto Sculpture Garden
MAP L4 ▪ 115 King St E
Rotating exhibits of contemporary site-specific works.

5 Red Canoe
MAP H5 ▪ Canoe Landing Park
A huge canoe sits atop a mound with views over the Gardiner Expressway.

6 Search Light, Star Light, Spot Light
MAP K5 ▪ Scotiabank Arena
Three hollow metal columns are pierced by hundreds of stars lit from within.

7 Mountain
MAP J4 ▪ Simcoe Park
This layered aluminum sculpture, cut with water jets, is by Anish Kapoor.

8 The Audience
MAP J5
"Fans" spill out of the Rogers Centre in this frieze by Michael Snow.

9 Woodpecker Column
MAP J5 ▪ 222 Bremner Blvd
Woodpeckers strike at this 100-ft (30-m) column.

10 City People
MAP K4 ▪ Royal Bank Plaza
Colorful figures spin softly in the breeze.

🔟 Green Spaces

1 High Park

Several miles of bicycle and walking trails meander through formal gardens, wooded ravines, and a rare oak savanna habitat in downtown's largest park *(see p98)*. At the south end is Colborne Lodge and Grenadier Pond, where locals fish in summer and skate in winter.

High Park, downtown's green oasis

2 Mount Pleasant Cemetery
MAP D1

The beautiful array of trees – many magnificently old and stately – in this cemetery dating from 1876 qualifies it as a bona fide arboretum. A walk through the lovely grounds will reveal the graves of several notable Canadians, including pianist Glenn Gould (1932–82), whose marker is carved with the opening bars of Bach's *Goldberg Variations*.

3 Leslie Street Spit
MAP F6

This area is officially known as the Outer Harbour East Headland. The northern half, designated as a nature reserve, is a man-made peninsula extending 3 miles (5 km) into Lake Ontario. More than 290 bird species have been seen here, and its forests, wetlands, and meadows contain rare plants. A lighthouse at the southern tip is a popular cyclist's destination.

4 Edwards Gardens
MAP B1

Flowerbeds of rhododendrons make this formal oasis popular in summer, especially for wedding parties. The Teaching Garden lets kids learn hands-on about nature. The Toronto Botanical Garden *(see p98)*, a horticultural center, is also here.

5 Yorkville Park
MAP C3

This gem packs a punch within its borders. It is divided into a series of gardens, each with a different theme, such as aspen grove, wetland, and meadow. Jets of mist rise at intervals around conifers; the enormous chunk of Canadian Shield granite makes a perfect perch for a rest.

6 Humber Bay Park East
MAP A2

Views of the city don't get much better than those from here. Easily accessible by bike on the Waterfront Trail, the park is also great for those on foot. A major habitat restoration, including wild flower meadow plantings, attracts birds and butterflies *(see p98)*, while walkways and interpretive signs complement a series of stormwater cleansing ponds.

7 Toronto Music Garden

This is one of the city's most unusual gardens *(see p67)*. Each of its six sections is inspired by a movement of Bach's *First Suite for Unaccompanied Cello*. The swirling paths, hills, and groves are dazzling.

8 Evergreen Brick Works

Nature and a city park have reclaimed the quarry of this former brickworks (see p89). Ponds and meadows of what is known as Weston Quarry Gardens attract birds and wildlife. Stop by the excavated "wall" to see the fossils of the area's early flora and fauna and its geologic history; some of the layers of deposits are over a million years old.

9 Rouge National Urban Park

Spread across 31 sq miles (79 sq km) along the Rouge River, this park (see p98) was designated a National Urban Park in 2011, the first of its kind in Canada. You can easily spend a day exploring its diversity of wildlife and plants, including a lakeside marsh.

Chipmunk, Rouge National Urban Park

10 Ashbridges Bay Park
MAP B2

Enjoy a picnic at this lakeside park while watching boats, or play a game at the baseball diamond. At the north end, the Martin Goodman bike trail (see p98) meets the Beach boardwalk.

A path through Toronto Music Garden

TOP 10 SPECTATOR SPORTS

A Maple Leafs player at a game

1 Toronto Maple Leafs
MAP K5 ▪ Scotiabank Arena, 40 Bay St ▪ 416 703 5323
This NHL team inspires adoration.

2 Toronto Blue Jays
MAP J5 ▪ Rogers Centre, 1 Blue Jays Way ▪ 1-888-OK-GO-JAY
Member of baseball's American League.

3 Toronto Raptors
MAP K5 ▪ Scotiabank Arena, 40 Bay St ▪ 416 366 3865
Popular NBA team that delights fans.

4 Toronto Argonauts
MAP J5 ▪ Rogers Centre, 1 Blue Jays Way ▪ 416 341 2746
Canadian Football League team.

5 Toronto Rock
MAP K5 ▪ Scotiabank Arena, 40 Bay St ▪ 416 596 3075
Players of lacrosse, the country's official national sport.

6 Toronto FC
MAP A5 ▪ BMO Field, Exhibition Pl ▪ 416 360 4625
The city's Major League Soccer team.

7 Woodbine Race Track
MAP A1 ▪ 555 Rexdale Blvd ▪ 416 675 7223
Home of the Queen's Plate horse race.

8 Honda Indy
MAP A5 ▪ 416 588 7223
Canadian highlight of the IZOD Indy Car racing series at Exhibition Place.

9 Scotiabank Toronto Waterfront Marathon
MAP A5–F5 ▪ 416 944 2765
Boston Marathon qualifier along the shore and through the Don Valley.

10 Toronto Marlies
MAP A5 ▪ Ricoh Coliseum, Exhibition Pl ▪ 416 597 7825
This AHL team sends players to the NHL.

TOP10 Off the Beaten Path

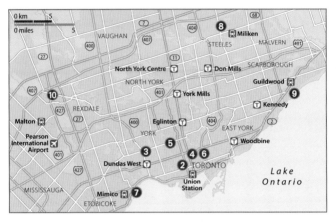

1 The Haunted Walk
www.hauntedwalk.com/
toronto-tours

This is a 90-minute walking tour of Toronto's darker past. Guides are local storytellers and amateur historians who share tales of ghostly encounters in downtown Toronto.

2 Graffiti Alley
MAP H4 ■ Enter at 753 Queen St W

South of Chinatown (see p77), Graffiti Alley is actually a series of connected alleyways. As the name suggests, it

Colorful street art, Graffiti Alley

is an urban canvas of vibrant street art created by talented local artists and used in many fashion shoots. It is best to go during daylight hours.

3 The Junction
MAP A2 ■ 20 Jerome St

In 1904, the residents of what was then a suburb voted to ban the sale of alcohol. The area remained dry until 1996. Today, at the corner of Dundas West and Keele Street, four century-old buildings rise from the ground. Head here for a mix of old and new, with chic bars, restaurants, shops, and a terracotta house.

4 Jarvis Street Mansions
MAP M1 ■ Jarvis St

To see where Toronto's elite once lived, check out the remaining grand homes along Jarvis Street. The Massey family (owners of a farm-equipment empire) called No. 515 home. Now a restaurant in the Keg chain, it is a designated heritage property, along with No. 519 Jarvis and two buildings on Wellesley Place.

5 Wychwood Park
MAP B1 ■ Entrance between 77 and 81 Alcina Ave

This late 19th-century enclave of gracious homes and tree-lined streets is a village within a big city. Founded as an artist's colony, it is now a private community managed by local residents. The public can enter through a little-known pedestrian passageway and wander through the grounds.

6 Toronto Necropolis
MAP E3 ■ 200 Winchester St, near Riverdale Farm

The Necropolis is the resting place of many of Toronto's famous citizens, including William Lyon Mackenzie, first mayor of Toronto and a leader of the Upper Canada Rebellion. The non-sectarian Gothic chapel is tranquil, and rare shrubs and Victorian monuments line the pathways.

7 Humber Bay Arch Bridge and Sheldon Lookout
MAP A2 ■ Martin Goodman Trail, south of Lakeshore Blvd W and near Windermere Ave

This arched pedestrian bridge sits at the mouth of the Humber River. Originally the start of an ancient First Nations trading route, it still features decorations that reflect the city's indigenous heritage. The bridge and the Sheldon Lookout to the west afford spectacular views of the city.

8 Pacific Mall
MAP B1 ■ 4300 Steeles Ave E ■ 905 470 8785

A wonderful slice of Asia in Toronto, Pacific Mall is said to be the largest indoor Chinese shopping center in North America. At the northeast end of the city, it stocks everything from electronics to hand-pulled noodles.

BAPS Shri Swaminarayan Mandir

9 Guild Park
MAP B1 ■ 201 Guildwood Parkway ■ www.todocanada.ca/city/toronto/listing/guildwood-park-gardens-scarborough-ontario

Toronto's most beloved architectural ruins lie at Guild Park, including old bank facades and columns, a school belfry, and other fragments of the city's rich architectural history. The park is located along the breathtaking Scarborough Bluffs.

Ancient ruins dotting Guild Park

10 BAPS Shri Swaminarayan Mandir
MAP A1 ■ 61 Claireville Dr ■ 416 798 2277 ■ www.baps.org

The BAPS Shri Swaminarayan Mandir is a traditional Hindu place of worship and an architectural masterpiece. It is made of 24,000 pieces of hand-sculpted Italian marble, and its extensive grounds include a Heritage Museum that is open to visitors. Modest attire is recommended to enter the premises.

Children's Attractions

1 Ripley's Aquarium of Canada

Children will love the huge tanks filled with all things marine, at this aquarium *(see pp28–9)*, especially the ones that have perspex bubbles and tunnels they can crawl into to be part of the display.

2 Hockey Hall of Fame

Budding hockey stars can test their skill whacking pucks and guarding goal at this shrine *(see pp32–3)* to the sport, which houses hockey memorabilia and exhibits.

Logo from the Hockey Hall of Fame

3 Ontario Science Centre

There will be no need to rein in the kids at this science-based learning playground *(see p95)*. Instead, you can let them charge through more than 800 hands-on exhibits encompassing everything from sports to medicine, and computers to electricity.

4 Harbourfront Centre

The kid-friendly attractions and events at this lakefront center *(see p67)* ensure it's always busy. Children especially love watching artisans at work in the Artport's Craft Studio, the ice-skating rink, and open-air concerts.

5 Young People's Theatre

This theater *(see p71)* presents excellent productions that are always a hit with kids. The facade of the original building, built in 1881 as a stable for street-car-pulling horses, can still be seen.

6 Centre Island

A major highlight of this Toronto Island is Centreville *(see p19)*, a retro amusement park. Some 30 old-fashioned rides include swan-shaped paddle boats, a lovely 1907 carousel, and even pony rides.

7 Canada's Wonderland

This amusement park *(see p95)* has 200 attractions, including over 69 rides, a water park, and live shows. There are plenty of thrilling rides for older kids, including one of the world's tallest roller coasters, Leviathan. Little ones will love the tamer rides, including a tug boat.

Families enjoying the Funway ride at Canada's Wonderland

Kids at the Royal Ontario Museum

8 Royal Ontario Museum

Canada's largest museum (see pp12–15) is a truly magical place for children. It makes a special effort to have plenty of hands-on exhibits. The Dinosaur Gallery and mummy cases are strictly "don't touch," but the Hands-On Biodiversity Gallery will enchant youngsters with its fun, interactive exhibits, as will the CIBC Discovery Room.

9 Riverdale Farm

MAP E3 ▪ 201 Winchester St
▪ Open 9am–5pm daily

This agricultural education center and working farm in the middle of the city is home to many barnyard favorites – pigs, goats, sheep, horses, and chickens. Its post-and-beam barns date from the 19th century. This is a re-creation of a working farm, and animals should not be petted.

10 Legoland Discovery Centre

Children can hone their building skills at a scaled-down version of a LEGO® theme park, located within an outlet mall. The Legoland Discovery Centre (see p97) hosts four fun rides – one of which is NINJAGO themed – as well as a 4-D movie theater, play areas, and a tour of the LEGO® factory.

TOP 10 PLACES TO EAT WITH KIDS

1 Sunset Grill
MAP J4 ▪ 2006 Queen St E,
The Beach ▪ 416 690 9985
Children love diners, and this is a particularly good one.

2 Wayne Gretzky's
MAP J4 ▪ 99 Blue Jays Way
▪ 416 979 7825
Pub fare and hockey memorabilia.

3 Five Doors North
MAP B2 ▪ 2088 Yonge St
▪ 416 480 6234
Classic Italian pastas and grilled meats.

4 Swiss Chalet
MAP J6 ▪ 266 Queens Quay W
▪ 416 596 7292
A kid-friendly, Canadian casual dining chain that serves ribs, fries, and more.

5 Stack
Dependable BBQ restaurant (see p99) with mini portions for children.

6 Magic Oven
MAP F3 ▪ 798 Danforth Ave
▪ 416 868 6836
Delicious pizza and pasta east of Pape.

7 Lakeview Restaurant
MAP A4 ▪ 1123 Dundas St W
▪ 416 535 2828
Old-style diner with retro menu.

8 La Cubana
MAP A2 ▪ 392 Roncesvalles Ave
▪ 416 538 7500
Familiy-friendly with a great patio.

9 Fancy Franks Gourmet Hot Dogs
MAP H2 ▪ 326 College St ▪ 416 920 3647
Wiener shop offering 18 signature all-beef hot dogs.

10 Old Spaghetti Factory
MAP L5 ▪ 54 The Esplanade
▪ 416 864 9761
A perennial favorite, great for groups.

Interior of Old Spaghetti Factory

🔟 Entertainment Venues

The spectacularly preserved auditorium at the Elgin Theatre

1 Elgin and Winter Garden Theatres

These two theaters have been restored to their original splendor. Opened in 1913 as a double-decker venue – with the Winter Garden seven stories above the Elgin (see p71) – they host concerts, operas, and hit Broadway musicals.

2 Koerner Hall

MAP C3 ■ 273 Bloor St W ■ 416 408 0208 ■ www.performance. rcmusica.ca

Part of the Royal Conservatory of Music's Telus Centre for Performing and Learning, Koerner Hall's acoustics are second to none. Enjoy jazz, classical, and World Music here.

3 Meridian Hall

MAP L5 ■ 1 Front St E ■ 1 855 872 7669 ■ www.sonycentre.ca

Famed dancer Mikhail Baryshnikov defected in Toronto from the Soviet Union in 1979. The refurbished theater mounts shows as diverse as Beck, Sesame Street Live, and the Eifman St. Petersburg Ballet.

4 Budweiser Stage

MAP A5 ■ 909 Lake Shore Blvd W ■ 416 260 5600 ■ www. canadianamphitheatre.net

With its lakeside setting, the Budweiser Stage is a great place for a summer concert. There's seating for 8,000 under the canopy, plus space for 8,000 more on the grass.

5 Toronto Centre for the Arts

MAP A1 ■ 5040 Yonge St ■ 416 250 3708 ■ www.tocentre.com

In surburban North York, the center's four stages host Broadway musicals, symphony orchestras, and well-known popular and classical singers.

6 Roy Thomson Hall

MAP J4 ■ 60 Simcoe St ■ 416 872 4255 ■ www.roythomson.com

This concert hall's innovative design ensures that everyone in the audience is within 100 ft (30 m) of the stage.

Music performance at Koerner Hall

7 St. Lawrence Centre for the Arts

MAP L5 ▪ 27 Front St E ▪ 416 366 7723 ▪ www.stlc.com

This venue presents theater, dance, and music, as well as lectures on subjects of topical interest, in its two intimate spaces – the larger Bluma Appel Theatre, and the Jane Mallet Theatre, which features recitals and performances by groups such as the Toronto Operetta Theatre Company.

8 Young Centre for the Performing Arts

MAP E5 ▪ 50 Tank House Lane ▪ 416 866 8666 ▪ www.youngcentre.ca

The performance space here is also the main venue for the George Brown Theatre School. It hosts a number of other local performances.

Four Seasons Centre lit up at night

9 Four Seasons Centre for the Performing Arts

MAP K4 ▪ 145 Queen St W ▪ COC: 416 363 8231; www.coc.ca ▪ NBC: 416 345 9595; www.national.ballet.ca

This large, beautiful space is home to two of Canada's most important performing arts companies – the Canadian Opera Company and the National Ballet of Canada.

10 Massey Hall

MAP L4 ▪ 178 Victoria St ▪ 416 872 4255 ▪ www.masseyhall.com

This grande dame built in 1894. Its 2,750 seats and superb acoustics provide a surprisingly intimate setting for jazz, blues, and folk shows.

TOP 10 PERFORMING ARTS GROUPS

National Ballet of Canada

1 National Ballet of Canada
MAP K4 ▪ national.ballet.ca
Internationally acclaimed company with the classics and new productions.

2 Tarragon Theatre
MAP B2 ▪ www.tarragontheatre.com
Performances of new innovative works by Canadian playwrights.

3 Tafelmusik
MAP C3 ▪ www.tafelmusik.org
The ensemble plays Baroque chamber music on period instruments.

4 Theatre Passe Muraille
MAP G3 ▪ passemuraille.ca
Theatre pioneers *(see p71)* that have shaped a distinctly Canadian voice.

5 Toronto Mendelssohn Choir
MAP B3 ▪ www.tmchoir.org
Canada's oldest vocal ensemble presented its first concert in 1895.

6 Toronto Symphony Orchestra
MAP J4 ▪ www.tso.ca
This renowned orchestra delights with the classics at the Roy Thomson Hall.

7 Canadian Stage
MAP E5 ▪ www.canadianstage.com
Productions of international and Canadian works, including musicals.

8 Canadian Opera Company
MAP K4 ▪ www.coc.ca
Largest producer of opera in Canada with seven productions each season.

9 Toronto Dance Theatre
MAP E3 ▪ www.tdt.org
Intelligent and visually striking modern dance by an influential dance troupe.

10 Soulpepper Theatre Company
MAP E5 ▪ www.soulpepper.ca
Interesting Canadian interpretations of international classics.

LGBT+ Venues

1 Club 120
MAP L4 ■ 120 Church St
■ www.club120.ca

Over two floors above a restaurant on the intersection of Church and Richmond streets, this upscale nightclub hosts a plethora of events, including T-Girl nights, open-mic comedy, and a monthly naked dance party TNT!MEN. On the weekends the crowds mix up and things get going with international DJs holding court late into the night. Check the website for the events schedule.

2 Barbara Hall Park
MAP L1 ■ 519 Church St

This popular meeting place, with its benches and greenery, is home to a permanent AIDS memorial, installed in 1993. The pillars are inscribed, upon request and with no geographic restrictions, with the names of those lost to the virus. The Universal Remembrance Plaque is a tribute to those who remain unnamed.

AIDS memorial, Barbara Hall Park

3 Woody's
MAP L1 ■ 467 Church St
■ 416 972 0887

A stuffed rhinoceros head presiding over the bar greets patrons at this local watering hole. A pool table and soft-core videos keep the clientele entertained, as do special events, such as the Best Chest contest, here and at sibling bar Sailor, next door.

Neon-illuminated Glad Day Bookshop

4 Glad Day Bookshop
MAP L1 ■ 499 Church St
■ 416 961 4161

Established in 1970 as Canada's first LGBT+ bookstore, Glad Day's excellent collection includes a wide selection of academic, fiction, and hard-to-find titles, as well as racy picture books and magazines. The used books section on the second floor is worth checking out.

5 Crews & Tangos
MAP L1 ■ 508 Church St
■ 637 349 7469

This is a fun spot to dance the night away to hip hop, R&B, top-40 hits, and the best local and NY-based DJs around. The crowd is mixed and welcoming. If you are after some theatricality, then this is the right place – they host a popular drag show every night.

6 Church Street
The intersection of Church and Wellesley streets has been the epicenter of Toronto's large LGBT+ community for decades. Excellent bars, restaurants, and specialty shops make the strip a great place

to soak up the scene, as leathermen, muscle boys, and drag performers strut their stuff. The 519 Community Centre hosts regular social events and gatherings, as well as offering a multitude of drop-in programs and short-term counseling.

7 The Beaver
MAP A4 ▪ 1192 Queen St W
▪ 416 537 2768

Head to this casual little café that turns into raucous fun from 11pm, featuring DJs that spin dancehall, hip hop, 1990s grunge, and even country. The Beaver also hosts karaoke on Sundays.

8 Hair of the Dog
MAP L2 ▪ 425 Church St
▪ 416 964 2708

A laid-back spot, Hair of the Dog serves standard pub fare alongside draft beer. The sizeable patio, located at the back and south facing, is the big draw here.

9 Hanlan's Point Beach
MAP B6

This secluded Toronto Island beach has the city's only official clothing-optional area (don't take off your clothes until you reach the fenced section at the south end). In 1999, it reclaimed its status as a nude beach *(see p19)*, as it was between 1894 and 1930, enabling nudists and cruisers to again bathe in the buff. There are "no swimming" signs when water pollution levels are high.

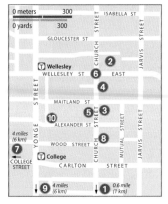

10 Buddies in Bad Times Theatre
MAP L1 ▪ 12 Alexander St ▪ 416 975 8555 ▪ www.buddiesinbadtimes.com

This groundbreaking company, set in Toronto's LGBT+ oriented village, established in 1979, is one of the world's oldest and largest venues for LGBT+ culture productions. In its history spanning several decades, Buddies in Bad has made its way into the hearts of over a million people. Renowned for innovative and edgy works, productions often push the boundaries of artistic convention and sometimes even propriety. On Saturdays at 10:30pm Tallulah's Cabaret takes over with DJs and wild dancing, and – true to its name – some kind of outrageous performance.

Buddies in Bad Times Theatre

🔟 Restaurants

1 Mildred's Temple Kitchen

Set in a post-industrial district of Victorian-era brick factories, Mildred's (see p83) features a menu of dishes created with seasonal produce. On weekends, try the Big Brunch Skillet of pulled pork, black beans, and eggs, or Veda's Choice (eggs Benedict on a croissant). The rosemary bacon is cured in-house.

2 Lady Marmalade

Among the best places for brunch in Leslieville. This restaurant (see p93) offers Mexican-inspired *huevos* and creative takes on eggs Benedict.

3 Lai Wah Heen

Serving exceptional Cantonese cuisine, this elegant two-level restaurant (see p83) in the DoubleTree by Hilton redefines classic Chinese fare. Elegant details include silver chopstick rests and starched linens on the round tables, which are suitable for large groups and conducive to sharing (smaller tables also available). The Sunday dim sum is particularly popular.

4 Chiado

Dine on the freshest fish and seafood to be had in the city, flown in from the world's wharfs daily and transformed into the most luxurious of Portuguese fare. The wine list here (see p99) is replete with unusual offerings, which the waitstaff are expert at elucidating and pairing with dishes. Try the tapas menu at the wine bar in the restaurant's modern annex addition, Senhor Antonio.

Blueberry pancakes at Aunties and Uncles

5 Aunties and Uncles

A charmingly eclectic eatery, Aunties and Uncles (see p83) is housed in a former 1950s barber shop. The soups, salads, omelets, and sandwiches here are excellent, and the juice is freshly squeezed. Almost every-thing is served with trademark sides of pea meal bacon and buttery challah toast.

6 Le Sélect Bistro

A much-loved Toronto mainstay, this bistro (see p73) has cane chairs on the patio, and a proper zinc bar. It serves all the popular weekend brunch options, Alsace classics including *choucroute*, as well as French favorites such as steak tartare, gigot d'agneau, and confit de canard that are prepared with regional ingredients.

French-style chic, Le Sélect Bistro

Contemporary setting at The Chase

(7) The Chase

Refined dining is on offer in a bright, window-walled penthouse (see p72) atop the Heritage listed Dineen Building. Carefully prepared dishes, such as lobster layered with truffles or chestnut and foie gras ravioli, allow the world-class food to sing. There's less formal dining in The Chase Fish and Oyster, which is located on the ground floor.

(8) Canoe

Stellar views from the 54th floor of the Toronto Dominion Bank Tower make this (see p73) one of the most enchanting eateries in the city. Lunchtime business crowds close deals over lobster club sandwiches on brioche, but the evening ambience is more romantic. Menu mainstays include Canadian elk and Quebec suckling pig.

(9) Noce

This intimate restaurant (see p83) serves marvelous Italian food, delivered with welcoming, friendly service. The homemade pasta specials are always superb, as are grilled and roasted meats. The summer patio is great for alfresco dining.

(10) Buca

This trendy basement *osteria* (see p73) is tucked up an alleyway beside the Scholastic building. The acclaimed, earthy Italian menu is based on the "nose-to-tail" philosophy of utilizing the entire animal in cooking. Fare includes unusual quirks such as bison prosciutto.

TOP 10 BEST CANADIAN SNACKS

1 Roasted Chestnuts
Sidewalk vendors sell steaming-hot, smoky-flavored roast chestnuts in summer and fall.

2 Poutine
Hailing from Québec, *poutine* (french fries topped with cheese curds and hot gravy) is now ubiquitous in Toronto.

3 Falafel
Deep-fried chickpea balls in pita pockets stuffed with *tahini* sauce, onion, and tomato.

4 Bubble Tea
An Asian concoction of sweet, flavored cold tea, milk, and tapioca pearls.

5 Gelato
More refreshing and lighter than ice cream, Italian ices come in a range of flavors, from lemon to caramel.

6 Corn on the Cob
Little India street vendors prepare grilled corn glazed with lemon juice and tangy spices.

7 Hot Dogs
Outdoor carts grill hot dogs, veggie dogs, and sausages. Polish sausage is piled high with all the fixings – pickles, hot mustard, and sauerkraut.

8 Jamaican Roti
Soft flat bread encases a variety of fillings, from curried goat or chicken to spinach and squash. The hot sauce is optional.

9 Churrasco Chicken
Spiked with tangy Portuguese *piri piri* sauce, then barbecued to perfection; served on a bun or with roasted spuds.

10 Chinese Buns
Steamed dough filled with savory meat, vegetables, or sweet coconut and red bean paste. Eat piping hot.

Chinese steamed buns

Bars and Clubs

A live band entertaining an audience at the Lula Lounge

1 Lula Lounge

Lively bands and popular DJs play everything Latin, from merengue to salsa here *(see p81)*. Enjoy dinner before the show, arrive later for drinks, or go all out with a dance lesson/ dinner show package.

2 The Bar at ALO

This classic bar *(see p83)*, with gracious staff, is on the third floor of a Victorian building. The food is several cuts above the usual, with small plates of dishes such as sashimi or rack of pork. Cocktails (try the Armagnac old-fashioned) are served with panache.

The Bar at ALO with a range of drinks

3 Bar Hop

The bars that sold proper cask-pulled beer were few and far between a decade ago, but Toronto has finally joined the craft beer renaissance. Bar Hop *(see p72)* is among the best, regularly bringing in guest beers to join its 36 taps.

4 d|bar

It's all about style at this busy see-and-be-seen bar *(see p81)* on the first floor of the prestigious Four Seasons Hotel in fashionable Yorkville. Adept servers prepare the perfect cocktail in a miniature shaker at your table; nary a drop is spilled. At the bar, business tycoons talk takeovers while scoping out the room.

5 Pravda Vodka House

Decked out in gold and red Russian furnishings, with portraits of Stalin and Lenin on the walls, this bar *(see p92)* serves up more than 70 of the world's best vodkas.

6 The Fifth Social Club

The loft-style dance club of this restaurant/bar venue *(see p72)* caters to the 25-plus crowd. Bouncers ignore the jeans-clad in favor of those in casual-smart attire. Inside, grab a drink at one of four bars, then dance to R&B and top-40 music.

⑦ Cameron House

Giant "ants" on the front of this former flophouse signal a different bar experience *(see p81)*. Notable for the acts that played here before making it big, this low-key bar is dedicated to up-and-coming musicians. Join foot-stomping regulars on weekends for pay-what-you-can country music.

⑧ The Roof Lounge

A haunt of creative types, this bar *(see p81)* located atop the Park Hyatt Hotel offers refuge from daily stresses. In winter, a fireplace and leather chairs beckon; in summer, spectacular views from the terrace.

⑨ Irish Embassy Pub & Grill

Pub lovers will feel at home at this pub *(see p72)* with the mahogany bar, and the stool and booth seating set among the marble columns of this historic bank building. Good choice of beers on tap, and tasty pub food.

Irish Embassy Pub & Grill

⑩ Bar at Canoe

On the 54th floor of the TD Bank Tower *(see p68)*, this sophisticated spot *(see p72)* caters to corporate wheelers and dealers (reduced to size against the magnificent view of Lake Ontario). There's an excellent selection of wines, cocktails, and beers. Note that the bar is closed on weekends.

TOP 10 VENUES FOR LIVE MUSIC

Mood lighting at Adelaide Hall

1 Adelaide Hall
MAP J4 ▪ 250 Adelaide St W
Great intimate venue for indie bands and other acts, in the heart of the city.

2 Rivoli
MAP H4 ▪ 334 Queen St W
Booking top alternative rock bands has made this spot a Toronto landmark.

3 Danforth Music Hall
MAP F3 ▪ 147 Danforth Ave
Originally a cinema, this mid-size venue has a balcony and slanted floors.

4 Horseshoe Tavern
MAP H4 ▪ 368 Queen St W
A stalwart of Queen West since 1947, showcasing the best of Toronto bands.

5 Opera House
MAP F4 ▪ 735 Queen St E
An eclectic range of bands plays beneath the ornate proscenium arch. All-ages shows and blues nights pack the place.

6 The Rex Hotel
MAP J3 ▪ 194 Queen St W
The hotel's jazz and blues bar attracts Canada's finest musicians.

7 Hugh's Room
MAP A4 ▪ 2261 Dundas St W
Enjoy a range of musical genres in a wonderfully intimate space.

8 Lee's Palace
MAP B3 ▪ 529 Bloor St W
This gritty joint hosts edgy rock bands.

9 Reservoir Lounge
MAP L4 ▪ 52 Wellington St E
Swing-jazz, jump blues, and southern fusion cuisine. Closed Sunday.

10 Phoenix Concert Theatre
MAP M1 ▪ 410 Sherbourne St
Rock bands, and dancing on DJ theme nights.

⏣ Toronto for Free

Entrance to the Thomas Fisher Library

① Unusual Libraries
Thomas Fisher Library: MAP J1; 120 St. George St; 416 978 5285 ■ Merril Collection of Science Fiction, Speculation & Fantasy: MAP H2; 239 College St; 416 393 7748
Part of the University of Toronto but open to the public, the Thomas Fisher Rare Book Library houses around 700,000 volumes. The Merril Collection is intriguing, offering more than 70,000 books in categories such as parapsychology and UFOs.

② Visit the Legislature
Tours: www.ola.org/en/visit-learn/tour-options
Visitors can take a variety of free tours (from 8:30am to 4:30pm most days) that provide glimpses into the province's Parliament. Themes include the Legislature's history and the architecture of the historic building (see p78) that houses it. Booking ahead of your visit is recommended.

Ice skating at Nathan Phillips Square

③ Don Valley Brick Works Park
MAP E2 ■ 550 Bayview Ave ■ 416 392 2489
A great example of Toronto's practice of reforming decrepit industrial lots into thriving green spaces. This park is popular for hiking and biking trails, farmers' markets as well as public art installations.

④ Walking Tours
Tour Guys: www.tourguys.ca/toronto ■ Heritage Canada: www.heritagetoronto.org/programs/tours
Tour Guys offers several free walking tours of Toronto, with themes such as history, food, and graffiti. To learn more about Toronto's architectural heritage try one of the free tours offered by Heritage Canada.

⑤ Concerts
Canadian Opera Company: www.coc.ca/performancesandtickets/freeconcertseries.aspx
The COC offers free indoor concerts most Tuesdays and Thursdays (Sep–Jun), with occasional performances on Wednesdays. Free outdoor performances take place in summer.

⑥ Ice Skating in Winter
MAP K3 ■ www.nathanphillips squareskaterentals.com
During winter, the reflecting pool in Nathan Phillips Square becomes a popular ice-skating rink. Visitors without skates of their own can rent a pair on site for a small fee.

7 Watch a Movie Being Made

ACTRA Toronto: www.actratoronto.com/whats-shooting

ACTRA lists the major productions currently being filmed on location in the city, so visitors can head down and experience the making of a major motion picture firsthand.

8 Museums and Galleries

Many museums, such as the Aga Khan Museum (see p96), offer a peek into the world's history through free entry at certain times. Art Gallery of Ontario (see pp20–21), which holds an extensive collection of fine art and modern sculpture spanning the first century to present day, and offers free admission to all visitors 25 and under.

Gallery at the Aga Khan Museum

9 Live Studio Audiences

CBC Broadcasting Centre: MAP J5; 250 Front St W; cbchelp.cbc.ca

Information on the popular CBC programs that allow visitors to be part of a live studio audience for free can be found on the CBC website. Advance booking is key.

10 Summer Outdoor Films

City Cinema: MAP L3; Yonge-Dundas Sq; www.ydsquare.ca/city-cinema.html ■ Free Flicks: MAP J6; Harbourfront; www.harbourfront centre.com/freeflicks09/index.cfm

Toronto loves its cinema, with plenty of free film showings to be found in the city. City Cinema offers free films (mostly frothy comedies) on Tuesdays at sunset. For crowd-pleasing movies, try Free Flicks at Harbourfront on Wednesdays at dusk.

TOP 10 BUDGET TIPS

Summer waterfront festival

1 Throughout summer, a multitude of free events, such as concerts, food festivals, and dancing on the pier, are held at Harbourfront (see p67).

2 CityPass (www.citypass.com/toronto) gives substantial discounts to a collection of attractions including the CN Tower (see pp16–17) and Casa Loma (see pp24–5). This booklet is valid for 9 consecutive days, starting from the first day that you use it.

3 Buy a day pass from a subway boot if you're planning on making multiple trips; they offer real savings.

4 Several parks and beaches (www.toronto.ca.parks) offer outdoor gyms, as well as grills and picnic tables.

5 Many hotels offer discounts when booked online. Members of auto clubs and AARP (American Association of Retired Persons) often get discounts.

6 Buffet lunches are popular and provide good value. At Dhaba Indian buffet (309 King Street West) there are more than 60 items to choose from for less than $15.

7 The city's board-game cafés, such as Snakes and Lattés (600 Bloor Street West) and C'est What (67 Front Street East), offer plenty of old-fashioned fun for around $5.

8 Tourism Toronto (www.seetorontonow.com) usually has good deals on packages for short stays throughout the year.

9 Toronto Islands (see pp18–19) provide a relaxing day's entertainment for the cost of a ferry ride.

10 The Travellers' Aid booth in Union Station can provide details on good budget accommodations.

🔟 Festivals

Visitors gather for a performance at North By Northeast (NXNE)

1 Hot Docs
Late Apr ▪ www.hotdocs.ca

This 11-day festival is dedicated to the art of documentary film-making, with around 200 films from Canada and across the world screened in 16 venues across the city.

2 Contact
May ▪ www.scotiabank contactphoto.com

The largest festival dedicated to photography in the world, Contact brings together over 1,500 artists to exhibit at 175 venues in the city. Big names round out the program along with retrospectives of the greats.

3 Luminato
Jun ▪ www.luminato festival.com

An internationally acclaimed multi-arts festival that takes place over 10 days, Luminato brings out the cutting-edge big hitters – think Rufus Wainwright recreating Judy Garland's 1961 Carnegie Hall show. The festival offers music galore, both local and international, as well as dance performances and talks by the likes of musicians David Byrne, Joni Mitchell, and Buffy Sainte-Marie. There are also many free events and even some stuff for kids.

4 NXNE
Jun ▪ www.nxne.com

It began as a grungy music event, but North By Northeast is now a cultural extravaganza encompassing film, art, talks, and new technology, and it takes over the downtown core for 10 days. Get your wristband and get out there – it's still an unbeatable chance to discover new bands.

5 Pride Week
Late Jun ▪ www.pride toronto.com

Toronto's Pride celebrations are legendary. Performances, music, and parties take over the Village around Church and Wellesley for 10 days. Three parades make sure all are represented – the Dyke March, Trans Parade, and the Pride Parade.

Revelers during Pride Week

⑥ Caribbean Carnival
Jul–early Aug ▪ www. torontocaribbeancarnival.com

A three-week extravaganza that celebrates all things Caribbean. The revelry culminates on the August long weekend with a huge parade, packed with elaborate costumes, along Lakeshore Boulevard.

⑦ Beaches International Jazz Festival
Late Jul ▪ www.beachesjazz.com

A free festival with mostly Canadian headliners, a Big Band Stage, and a Latino Stage. Over 40 bands play along Queen East – the crowds bring the neighborhood to a standstill.

⑧ SummerWorks
Aug ▪ www.summerworks.ca

This 10-day festival of performance is run by SummerWorks, known for forward-thinking Canadian theater. It is Canada's biggest juried festival.

Actor Benedict Cumberbatch at TIFF

⑨ TIFF
Sep ▪ www.tiff.net

Showcasing over 300 films from as many as 60 countries, the Toronto International Film Festival draws stars, independent film-makers, and movie buffs to the city for 10 days in early September.

⑩ Nuit Blanche
Early Oct ▪ www.scotiabank nuitblanche.com

An all-night contemporary arts festival, with over 100 art events scattered across town. Stay up until dawn – it can get pretty interesting.

TOP 10 FAMILY EVENTS

1 Sugarbush Maple Syrup Festival
Mar–Apr ▪ www.maple syrupfest.com
Learn how to make maple syrup.

2 TIFF Kids
Apr ▪ www.tiff.net
The best in contemporary and classic children's film is screened here.

3 Dragon Boat Race Festival
Jun ▪ www.dragonboats.com
Teams from around the world compete in a race at Centre Island.

4 Redpath Waterfront Festival
Jun–Jul ▪ www.towaterfrontfest.com
Fun along the shore: treasure hunts, a flyboarding competition, and dog trials.

5 Canada Day
Jul 1
Free concerts, activities, and fireworks at Mel Lastman Square.

6 Canadian National Exhibition
Mid-Aug–Labour Day (first Mon in Sep) ▪ www.theex.com
Themed pavilions, fairground amusements, and an air show.

7 Buskerfest
Sep ▪ www.torontobuskerfest.com
Acrobats, musicians, and lots more take over Yonge between Queen and College.

8 Word on the Street
Sep ▪ www.thewordonthestreet.ca
Literary festival with readings by popular authors.

9 Royal Agricultural Winter Fair
Nov ▪ www.royalfair.org
Country fair with horse jumping and livestock competitions.

10 Santa Claus Parade
Mid-Nov ▪ www.thesanta clausparade.ca
Toronto tradition featuring marching bands, floats, and the big man himself.

Dragon Boat Race Festival

Toronto
Area by Area

Aerial view of the Toronto skyline with
the Toronto Islands in the foreground

TOP 10 Harbourfront and the Financial District

Harbourfront and the Financial District combine old and new in a vibrant mix. Along the shores of Lake Ontario, the origins of the city can be traced to the establishment of Fort York in 1793. As the town of York grew, spreading north, financial institutions settled around Bay and King streets. High-rises and historic buildings are dotted throughout the area, while vaudeville theaters anchor an exuberant entertainment scene.

'The Audience' by Toronto artist Michael Snow, Rogers Centre

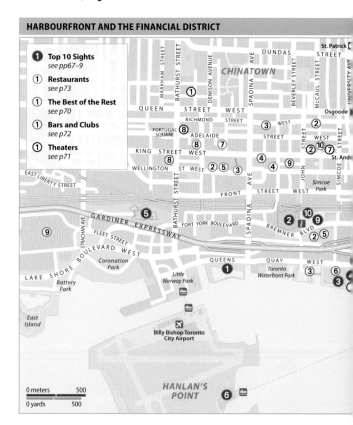

HARBOURFRONT AND THE FINANCIAL DISTRICT

1 **Top 10 Sights**
see pp67–9

① **Restaurants**
see p73

① **The Best of the Rest**
see p70

① **Bars and Clubs**
see p72

① **Theaters**
see p71

Rectital at the Toronto Music Garden

1 Toronto Music Garden
MAP H6 ▪ 475 Queens Quay W
▪ 416 973 4000 ▪ www.harbourfront
centre.com/summermusic

This elegant garden, a collaboration between famed cellist Yo Yo Ma, landscape architect Julie Moir Messervy, and city landscape architects, was inspired by Bach's *First Suite for Unaccompanied Cello*. Each movement in the suite – allemande, courante, sarabande, menuets, and gigue – plus a prelude, is represented by the plantings in one of the six sections of the garden. Concerts run from July through September.

2 Rogers Centre
MAP J5 ▪ 1 Blue Jays Way
▪ 416 341 1000

At the base of the CN Tower, this sports and large-events venue is home to the city's baseball team, the Blue Jays, and football team, the Argonauts. When built in 1989, it had the world's only fully retractable roof of its kind. When teams are not in action, you can tour the facility. Outside, a frieze by Toronto artist Michael Snow depicts 14 spectators.

3 Harbourfront Centre
MAP K6 ▪ 235 Queens Quay W
▪ 416 973 4000 ▪ Open 10am–11pm Mon–Sat (until 9pm Sun) ▪ www.harbourfrontcentre.com

This centre provides a wide range of recreational and cultural activities, and the Bill Boyle Artport is its fulcrum. Watch glass blowing in the craft studios, or admire the contemporary Canadian art at the Artport Gallery. The Brigantine Room hosts readings, workshops, as well as theater performances.

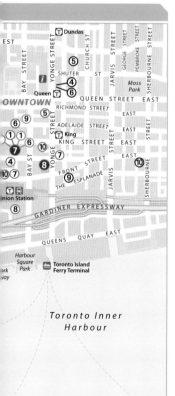

Harbourfront Centre

4 Queen's Quay Terminal

MAP K6 ■ 207 Queens Quay W ■ 416 203 3269 ■ Open 10am–6pm daily

In a converted 1927 building, this is a mix of condos, offices, and a retail complex bursting with boutiques that sell unusual gift items. Good food is on offer at its restaurants, many with patios overlooking the water. Harbor cruises depart from the terminal.

Condos at Queen's Quay Terminal

5 Fort York

MAP G5 ■ 250 Fort York Blvd ■ 416 392 6907 ■ Open early Sep–late May: 10am–4pm Mon–Fri, 10am–5pm Sat & Sun; late May–early Sep: 10am–5pm daily ■ Closed for special events ■ Adm

Established in 1793 to protect the growing city, this was the site of the Battle of York during the War of 1812, when the US invaded Upper Canada. The fort houses the country's largest collection of War of 1812 buildings, which display historic military items. Guides in costume give period music, musket, and drill demonstrations.

Canada Day at Fort York

CANADA'S WAR AGAINST THE US

On June 18, 1812, the US declared war on Great Britain and, for many months, battled at various border outposts such as Detroit and Queenston Heights. In April 1813, American troops invaded and occupied York (as Toronto was then called), burning the Parliament and destroying much of Fort York. The US won the Battle of York, but they soon abandoned the town to fight battles in the Niagara Peninsula. The American war with Britain ended in stalemate on December 24, 1814, with the signing of the Treaty of Ghent.

6 Toronto Islands

Recreational opportunities abound on the car-free islands (see pp18–19), from sunbathing and cycling to children's amusement rides. Ferries depart regularly for the islands from the foot of Bay Street; the 10-minute trip across the harbor offers unparalleled views of downtown.

7 Toronto-Dominion Centre

MAP K4 ■ 55 King St W

This six-tower complex is one of the most important pieces of architecture in the city (see p45). The black steel I-beams of the 1968 Toronto Dominion Bank Tower are trademark Mies van der Rohe (1886–1969), and perfectly reflect the famed architect's modernist dictum "Less is More." In the courtyard, seven bronze cow sculptures by Joe Fafard represent the roots of Canada's agrarian economy. Below ground is a shopping mall, the only one van der Rohe ever designed.

8 Hockey Hall of Fame

Hockey fans will be fascinated by the memorabilia in this museum *(see pp32–3)* dedicated to Canada's favorite sport. Everything from masks personalized by goalies to hand-carved skates from the 1840s reflect the history of the game. Have your photo taken with the iconic Stanley Cup, then test your skills at the game at the interactive exhibits.

9 Ripley's Aquarium of Canada

This state-of-the-art aquarium *(see pp28–9)* at the base of the CN Tower features over 16,000 marine animals in 50 exhibits, with a capacity of 1.5 million US gallons (5.7 million liters) of water. The Dangerous Lagoon features three different types of shark and has North America's longest underwater viewing tunnel at 315 ft (96 m).

Viewing tunnel, Ripley's Aquarium

10 CN Tower

Soaring 1,815 ft (553 m) above downtown, this is the defining icon *(see pp16–17)* of the city's skyline and the tallest building in the Western Hemisphere. Check out the state-of-the-art theater showing short but thrilling 3-D movies, then let a glass-fronted elevator zip you, in less than a minute, up to one of four lookout levels. Access to the SkyPod, which costs extra, is via a separate elevator. The experience is vertiginous and tends to be rather cramped. The popular revolving 360 Restaurant *(see p17)*, offers a view that changes slowly throughout the meal.

AN ART WALK

▶ MORNING

Start at **Commerce Court North** *(see p70)* and admire the stunning lobby. Walk west along King Street, just past Bay Street and the TD Centre. Note the courtyard cows, part of Joe Fafard's sculpture *The Pasture (see p45)*, on the lawn behind 77 King Street W. Just around the corner at 234 Bay Street is the **Design Exchange** *(see p70)*, former home of the Toronto Stock Exchange. Admire the metallic Art Deco doors featuring icons from industries from the 1930s, then head north up Bay Street to **Locale Mercatto** *(see p73)* for an Italian lunch.

AFTERNOON

Zigzag your way to **Simcoe Park**, on Front Street west of Simcoe, and admire the Anish Kapoor sculpture *Mountain (see p45)*. Continue west along Front, past the **CBC** *(see p61)*, noting the Glenn Gould sculpture, honoring the eccentric pianist. You'll soon come to the **Rogers Centre** *(see p67)*, and *The Audience*, Michael Snow's larger-than-life fans *(see p45)*. Turn left on Spadina Avenue; crossing the bridge, look left to see Eldon Garnet's memorial commemorating Chinese laborers who helped build Canada's railroads. Continue south down Spadina turning right onto Fort York Boulevard, where you'll find Canoe Landing Park. Head back to Spadina from where it's only 5 minutes to the lake and, just west on Queens Quay, the lovely **Toronto Music Garden** *(see p67)*.

See map on pp66–7

The Best of the Rest

Better Knowing, an exhibit by KAWS at the Design Exchange

1 Design Exchange
MAP K4 ■ 234 Bay St ■ Open 10am–5pm Mon–Fri, noon–5pm Sat & Sun ■ Adm (for special exhibits)

A design museum dedicated to showcasing Canadian postwar design.

2 Toronto Railway Museum
MAP J5 ■ 255 Bremner Blvd ■ Open noon–5pm Wed–Sun ■ Adm

Rolling stock and diesel and steam engines stand proud on the turntable of the John Street Roundhouse. Enjoy miniature train rides in summer.

3 401 Richmond Street
MAP H4 ■ 401 Richmond St W

Many of the city's best artist-run galleries are based in this gorgeous old warehouse. Find great gifts and reading material at Swipe Design ǀ Books + Objects.

4 Toronto Dominion Gallery of Inuit Art
MAP K4 ■ 79 Wellington St W ■ Open 8am–6pm Mon–Fri, 10am–4pm Sat & Sun

An outstanding collection (see p43) of postwar Inuit sculpture.

5 Steam Whistle Brewing
MAP J5 ■ 255 Bremner Blvd ■ Open 11am–6pm Mon–Sat, 11am–5pm Sun

This railroad roundhouse now functions as a microbrewery. Tour the facilities, then sample the beer.

6 Power Plant Contemporary Art Gallery
MAP K6 ■ 231 Queens Quay W ■ Open 10am–5pm Tue–Sun (until 8pm Thu); holiday Mondays

Toronto's premier contemporary art public gallery (see p42).

7 Fairmont Royal York
MAP K5 ■ 100 Front St W

Once the largest in the British Commonwealth, this grand château-style hotel (see p116) was built in 1928 by the Canadian Pacific Railway.

8 Scotiabank Arena
MAP K5 ■ 40 Bay St

Home to basketball's Raptors and hockey's Maple Leafs, the arena is in the old Toronto Postal Delivery Building. Carvings on the facade show the history of communications.

9 Exhibition Place
MAP A5

Princes' Gates herald the entrance to the Canadian National Exhibition's fairgrounds, hosting events such as the Royal Agricultural Winter Fair.

10 Commerce Court North
MAP L4 ■ 25 King St W

The star among Toronto's early skyscrapers, this massive 34-story Romanesque structure housing the Canadian Imperial Bank of Commerce was the tallest building in Canada when completed in 1931.

Theaters

1 Theatre Passe Muraille
MAP G3 ■ 16 Ryerson Ave
■ 416 504 7529

A great venue, Passe Muraille *(see p53)* has presented innovative productions since the 1960s, when it launched works developed by actors.

2 Princess of Wales Theatre
MAP J4 ■ 300 King St W ■ 416 872 1212

This venue for hit musicals opened in 1993, and was the first privately developed large theater the city had seen since 1907. The interior, by Toronto firm Yabu Pushelberg, spares no expense. Wall and ceiling murals are by American minimalist Frank Stella.

3 Fleck Dance Theatre
MAP K6 ■ 207 Queens Quay W
■ 416 973 4000

The *crème de la crème* of modern dance, by both local and visiting companies, has graced this stage.

4 Elgin Theatre
MAP L3 ■ 189 Yonge St ■ 1 855 622 2787 (tickets), 416 314 2871 (tours)

The lower half of the double-decker Elgin *(see p52)* and Winter Garden Theatre Centre was built in 1913 as a movie house and features lavish gilding and a proscenium arch.

5 Ed Mirvish Theatre
MAP L3 ■ 244 Victoria St
■ 416 872 1212

Musicals have replaced vaudeville on the bill. The 1920s interior is a fantasy of gilt-framed mirrors, chandeliers, an epic staircase, and dome.

6 Winter Garden Theatre
MAP L3 ■ 189 Yonge St ■ 1 855 622 2787 (tickets); 416 314 2871 (tours)

High above Elgin Theatre this room *(see p52)* is aptly named. On the ceiling, some 5,000 beech leaves glitter in the lantern light.

7 Royal Alexandra Theatre
MAP J4 ■ 260 King St W ■ 416 872 1212

Saved from demolition, this theater has been returned to Edwardian finery and features a dramatic mural.

The Royal Alexandra's stunning stage

8 Factory Theatre
MAP G4 ■ 125 Bathurst St
■ 416 504 9971

One of Toronto's oldest houses shows works by Canadian playwrights.

9 Bluma Appel Theatre
Devoted fans of Canada Stage's contemporary drama fill the seats in this theater *(see p53)*.

10 Young People's Theatre
MAP M4 ■ 165 Front St E
■ 416 862 2222 ■ www. youngpeoplestheatre.ca

An award-winning theater *(see p50)* that produces innovative plays for young viewers.

Ed Mirvish Theatre

See map on pp66–7

Bars and Clubs

1 Bar at Canoe
MAP K4 ▪ 66 Wellington St W
▪ 416 364 0054 ▪ Closed Sat & Sun

It's a heady experience sipping the perfect martini while gazing at the city from the top of a skyscraper. Bar at Canoe (see p59) is the place to come for after-work power drinks.

2 The Fifth Social Club
MAP J4 ▪ 225 Richmond St W (enter via alley) ▪ 416 979 3000 ▪ Closed Sun–Thu ▪ Adm

Popular nightclub (see p58) across two floors with original live shows and monthly theme parties. Head here for R&B and top 40 hits.

3 Amsterdam BrewHouse
MAP J6 ▪ 245 Queens Quay W
▪ 416 504 1020

The oldest craft brewery in the city, it concocts over 80 types of beer a year. Visit for a pint and great food.

4 Bar Hop
MAP H4 ▪ 391 King St W
▪ 647 352 7476

This place takes craft beer seriously. Choose from the 36 taps or from the seven-page beer menu.

5 The Chase
MAP L4 ▪ 10 Temperance St
▪ 647 346 7000

Take the elevator to the fifth floor of this heritage building and be dazzled by the polished, unpretentious service and sophisticated surroundings.

6 Cactus Club
MAP K4 ▪ First Canadian Pl, 77 Adelaide St W ▪ 647 748 2025

Drinks at the Cactus Club include innovative creations such as a decadent take on a martini. The contemporary art on display is impressive.

7 Irish Embassy Pub & Grill
Map L5 ▪ 49 Yonge St ▪ 416 866 8282

Savor a drink at the mahogany bar or delicious pub food at one of the comfortable banquettes (see p59).

8 Wheat Sheaf Tavern
MAP G4 ▪ 667 King St W
▪ 416 504 9912

Toronto's oldest tavern dates back to 1849. Enjoy chicken wings and a pint with TV sports, or go out on the deck.

9 Maison Mercer
MAP J4 ▪ 15 Mercer St
▪ 416 341 7777

This club pulls in some big name DJs. The brilliant roof terrace is open in summer.

10 Library Bar
MAP K5 ▪ 100 Front St W
▪ 416 860 5004

Tucked inside the Fairmont Royal York hotel (see p70), this bar has a gentleman's-club atmosphere, with its book-lined walls and leather chairs. The cocktails are great.

The sophisticated bar at The Chase

Restaurants

 Canoe
MAP K4 ▪ 66 Wellington St W
▪ 416 364 0054 ▪ Closed Sat & Sun ▪ $$$
Upscale Canadian dishes *(see p57)*
are the order of the day from chef
John Horne. The views from the
54th-floor room are stunning.

Marben's industrial-style interior

 Bymark
MAP K4 ▪ 66 Wellington St W
▪ 416 777 1144 ▪ Closed Sun ▪ $$
Some of the freshest fish in town
and extravagant *foie gras* attract a
well-heeled crowd. Top selection
of boutique Californian wines.

 Jacob's & Co
MAP H4 ▪ 12 Brant St
▪ 416 366 0200 ▪ $$$
Dry-aged steaks are cooked to
perfection at this modern take
on the classic steak house.

8 **Buca**
MAP G4 ▪ 604 King St W
▪ 416 865 1600 ▪ $$
Italian fare with a contemporary
twist served by friendly staff.

9 **Locale Mercatto**
MAP K4 ▪ 330 Bay St ▪ 416
306 0467 ▪ Closed Sat L & Sun ▪ $$
Find home-cooked food and excellent
wines at this down-to-earth eatery.
Popular with locals on weekdays.

Seafood dish, Locale Mercatto

 Marben
MAP H4 ▪ 488 Wellington St W
▪ 416 979 1990 ▪ Closed Mon ▪ $$
With a fine selection of vegetarian
and meat dishes, Marben's serves
up delicious, creative cuisine.

3 **Rodney's Oyster House**
MAP H4 ▪ 469 King St W
▪ 416 363 8105 ▪ Closed Sun ▪ $$
Two dozen types of oysters
and grilled fish entice fans.

4 **Luckee**
MAP J4 ▪ 328 Wellington St W
▪ 416 935 0400 ▪ Closed Mon ▪ $$
Toronto's own superstar chef Susur
Lee applies his artistry to the ulti-
mate small-plate meal – dim sum.

5 **Le Sélect Bistro**
MAP H4 ▪ 432 Wellington St
West ▪ 416 596 6405 ▪ $$
A much-loved French restaurant with
classy curved booths. Good wine list.

10 **Byblos**
MAP J4 ▪ 11 Duncan St
▪ 647 660 0909 ▪ Closed L ▪ $$
With Stuart Cameron as head
chef, Byblos serves an impeccable
mix of Middle Eastern cuisine and
regional ingredients. Try the
octopus and the lamb dishes.

See map on pp66–7

⟨TOP 10⟩ Downtown

Toronto is a city of neighborhoods, each with a distinct identity and many with an ethnic flavor, making it one of the most multicultural North American cities. In Chinatown, vendors compete with shoppers for sidewalk space, and restaurants offer everything from take-out buns to sit-down banquets. The multicultural mix has its fullest expression in Kensington Market, where Jamaican patty shops rub shoulders with Portuguese fish shops. Farther west is Little Italy, centered on College Street, while the downtown core has the upscale shopping area of Yorkville and many fine cultural institutions.

Wood carving at the AGO

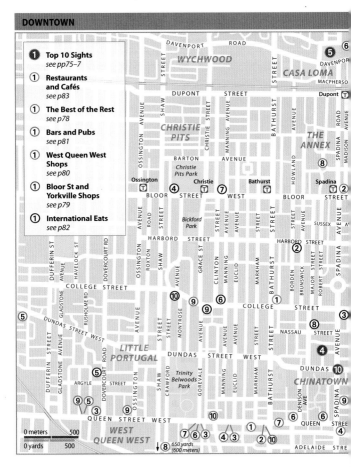

DOWNTOWN

- **1** Top 10 Sights
  see pp75–7
- **1** Restaurants and Cafés
  see p83
- **1** The Best of the Rest
  see p78
- **1** Bars and Pubs
  see p81
- **1** West Queen West Shops
  see p80
- **1** Bloor St and Yorkville Shops
  see p79
- **1** International Eats
  see p82

0 meters 500
0 yards 500

1 CF Toronto Eaton Centre

While it might seem strange that a shopping center is one of the most popular tourist attractions in the city – according to the numbers, at any rate – this retail complex *(see pp30–31)* is simply a very popular place to shop, meet, hang out, and people-watch, with crowds of boisterous teenagers attesting to this fact. Its massive size, with more than 300 stores, ensures that visitors can find practically anything they would want to buy here. Numerous restaurants, fast-food counters, and specialty treat shops round out the choices.

2 Art Gallery of Ontario

Particularly strong in historical and contemporary Canadian works, as well as host to important exhibitions, the AGO *(see pp20–21)* is one of the country's top art galleries.

The facade of Royal Ontario Museum

3 Royal Ontario Museum

Canada's premier museum *(see pp12–13)* has more than six million artifacts showcasing art, archeology, science, and nature.

4 Kensington Market
MAP H2

This funky neighborhood, in a small pocket west of Spadina, is the heart of multicultural Toronto – a place where vendors from across the globe have set up shop. An array of fruits, vegetables, and bulk dry goods spill out into the narrow sidewalks, while music blasts from open doors and loudspeakers. Pedestrians jostle with cyclists, and traffic moves at a snail's pace, especially on Saturdays. Leave the car behind and wander through the streets, soaking up the atmosphere. Try a Jamaican patty on Baldwin Street or browse vintage clothes at Exile *(62 Kensington Ave)* and contemporary fashion at Fresh Collective *(274 Augusta Ave)*.

Casa Loma, resembling a medieval castle, looming high above downtown

5 Casa Loma

This grand, castle-style mansion *(see pp24–5)* is a monument to the tastes and vision of Sir Henry Pellatt, a prominent financier, who, in 1911, commissioned renowned architect E. J. Lennox to build him a home. This immense architectural undertaking was on a scale never before seen in a private Canadian residence, with 98 rooms, 12 baths, 5,000 electric lights, and an elevator. Its $3.5 million cost helped bankrupt Sir Henry after he and his wife moved in, but its opulence remains in the extra-vagant rooms and fine furnishings.

Elton's platforms, Bata Shoe Museum

6 Bata Shoe Museum
MAP C3 ■ 327 Bloor St W
■ **Open 10am–5pm Mon–Sat, noon–5pm Sun** ■ **Adm**

This specialized museum *(see p42)*, founded by Sonia Bata, celebrates footwear form and function over the ages and around the world. Echoing a stylized shoebox, the building houses four galleries exhibiting everything from Roman sandals to Elton John's plat-forms. The exhibit of Chinese bound-foot shoes is definitely not for the squea-mish. The museum regularly holds interesting footwear-themed exhibitions.

7 Yorkville
MAP C3–D3

In the 1960s, this neighborhood was ground zero for hippies and youth culture; today, it is ground zero for establishment culture and the city's most upscale shopping *(see p79)*. Shops on Cumberland Street and Yorkville Avenue, between Bay Street and Avenue Road, sell cosmetics, jewelry, designer fashions, antiques, and leather luggage. Restaurants and bars cater to equally refined palates and wallets, and there are many fine-art galleries, exhibiting some of Canada's top names.

NATURAL AIR CONDITIONING

During the hot and humid days of a Toronto summer, Lake Ontario water does double duty. An innovative pro-ject utilizes the cold temperature of deep lake water – from intake pipes 270 ft (82 m) deep – to provide chilled energy for air conditioning Toronto's downtown high-rises and large facil-ities such as the Scotiabank Arena *(see p70)*. After the transfer of energy, the water is returned not to the lake but to the city's water-supply system, where it serves another crucial cooling function – as drinking water.

8 Campbell House

MAP K3 ■ 160 Queen St W
■ 416 597 0227 ■ Open 9:30am–4:30pm
Tue–Fri, noon–4:30pm Sat & Sun
(Jun–Aug: open Sun); closed Jan,
Good Fri–Easter Mon, Thanksgiving
weekend, Dec 25–31 ■ Adm

The city's oldest remaining building,
this Georgian mansion was built in
1822 for William Campbell, an Upper
Canada judge. In 1972, the building
was moved from its original location
on Adelaide Street to its present
spot, restored, and opened to the
public. Guided tours are available.

9 City Hall

MAP K3 ■ 100 Queen St

When City Hall (see p45) opened in
1965, the result of an international
design competition won by Finnish
architect Viljo Revell, the building
was highly controversial – the two
curving towers caused an uproar.
It has since become a prized landmark of the city, and the central
plaza, Nathan Phillips Square, a
lively symbol of civic life – a place for
political demonstrations, winter ice
skating, a summer farmers' market,
concerts, and celebrations. Inside
are murals and fabulous artworks.

10 Chinatown

MAP H2–H3

A steady flow of Chinese immigrants
keeps Toronto's Chinatown one of
the most vibrant in North America.
Hundreds of restaurants cater to all
tastes and budgets alongside shops
selling Oriental wares.

A vibrant street in Chinatown

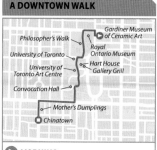

A DOWNTOWN WALK

▶ MORNING

Start the day at the **Gardiner
Museum of Ceramic Art** (see p78),
taking 90 minutes to peruse the
permanent collections and visiting exhibits. On your way out,
pop into the gift shop to have
a look at the unique crafts.

Head north to **Bloor Street** and
turn left, walking a half block to
the iron gates of Philosophers'
Walk, beside the **Royal Ontario
Museum** (see pp12–15). Take this
charming footpath, which follows
the course of the now-buried
Taddle Creek, exiting at Hoskin
Street in the heart of the **University
of Toronto** campus (see p78).
Wander south to the Late Gothic
Revival Hart House, lunching at
Gallery Grill (7 Hart House Circle).

AFTERNOON

After lunch, poke around the
stately common rooms and
library of Hart House, noting the
paintings throughout. Check out
the Canadian art on display at
Justina M. Barnicke Gallery, too.

From Hart House turn right
toward University College and
some of the most historic
buildings on campus. Stop by
the Laidlaw Wing to visit the
University of Toronto Art Centre
(see p43). Just to the south, on
King's College Circle, is the 1906
Convocation Hall, with its Ionic-
column-supported dome. Peek
inside if the doors are unlocked.

From here, head to a feast at
Mother's Dumplings (see p82)
in **Chinatown**, a couple of
blocks' stroll south and west.

See map on pp74–5

The Best of the Rest

 Gardiner Museum of Ceramic Art

MAP C3 ▪ 111 Queen's Park ▪ 416 586 8080 ▪ Open 10am–5pm Wed, Fri–Mon (until 9pm Thu) ▪ Adm

Historic and modern pieces from around the world can be seen at the Gardiner Museum (see p42).

 **Bloor Street**

MAP C3–D3

An upscale shopping strip of high-end fashion and home-decor stores, Bloor Street is a haven for shoppers.

3 University of Toronto

MAP H1–J1

A sprawling campus (see p44) of green spaces and historic stone buildings dominates a huge swath of the central city, fanning out north, east, and west from Queen's Park.

4 Old City Hall

MAP K3 ▪ 60 Queen St W

The entranceway columns carry carved caricatures of local politicians, with one exception – a straight-faced depiction of the architect. The edifice is now a courthouse (see p45).

5 Osgoode Hall

MAP K3 ▪ 130 Queen St W ▪ 416 947 3300 ▪ Open Aug–late Jun: 11:45am–2pm Mon–Fri

Ontario's first law school now houses upper provincial courts. The interior of the building is magnificent.

 Spadina Museum

MAP C2 ▪ 285 Spadina Rd ▪ Open Jan–mid-Apr: noon–5pm Sat & Sun; mid-Apr–Aug: noon–5pm Tue–Sun; Sep–Dec: noon–4pm Tue–Fri (until 5pm Sat & Sun) ▪ Adm

A restored 1866 house with exhibits from the 1920s to the 1940s. Tours only.

A preserved room, Spadina Museum

 West Queen West

MAP A4–B4

This neighborhood (see p80) has eclectic shops, galleries, and cafés.

 The Annex

MAP C2–C3

An upscale area with leafy sidestreets and lively restaurants, pubs, and shops north of Bloor Street makes The Annex perfect for a stroll.

9 Little Italy

MAP B3–B4

Shops and delis bustle all day long; bars and restaurants buzz at night.

10 Ontario Legislative Building

MAP K1 ▪ 1 Queen's Park ▪ Open mid-May–Aug: 8:30am–5:30pm daily; Sep–mid-May: 8:30am–4:30pm Mon–Fri

This stately building (see p60) is set in a park dotted with statues and cannons. Watch politicians in action from the gallery or join in a tour.

Trees in blossom in front of Osgoode Hall

Bloor Street and Yorkville Shops

 TNT (The New Trend)
MAP D3 ▪ 87 Avenue Rd

Yorkville Village's trendiest tenants attract the stylish set with their designer clothes. An adjacent, extension store, TNT Concept, opened in fall 2017.

2 Holt Renfrew
MAP D3 ▪ 50 Bloor St W

A world-class department store, Holt Renfrew features high fashion, as well as more affordable clothing, from its own label, perfumes and cosmetics, a hair salon, epicure store, café, and free personal shopping service.

3 George C
MAP C2 ▪ 21 Hazleton Ave

This store occupies a converted Victorian residence and stocks exclusive and contemporary high fashion for men and women. The selectively curated and reverently displayed pieces include exquisitely crafted boots by Rocco P and leather fashions by Drome.

4 Harry Rosen
MAP C3 ▪ 82 Bloor St W

Head-to-toe service is writ large at this menswear store featuring apparel from top design houses, including Canali and Hugo Boss. They stock suits, trousers, shirts, shoes, and accessories.

5 David's
MAP D3
▪ 66 Bloor St W

Shoe lovers will go wild among the stylish range of footwear from high-end designers here.

 Pusateri's
MAP D3 ▪ 57 Yorkville Ave

Food aficionados will love the luxury grocery items such as caviar and truffle oil, and flavorsome prepared foods.

Fashion goods displayed at Roots

 Roots
MAP C3 ▪ 80 Bloor St W

Quality sportswear, casual clothes, and leather goods for every member of the family are on offer from this popular Canadian brand.

8 L'Atelier Grigorian
MAP D3 ▪ 70 Yorkville Ave

The city's premier location for jazz, classical, and world music, L'Atelier Grigorian has been a regular stop for audiophiles passing through the city since 1980.

Delicious shortbread basket from Pusateri's

9 Liss Gallery
MAP C3 ▪ 112 Cumberland St

Cutting-edge exhibitions of contemporary paintings, photography, and sculptures are held here, often with the artist in attendance.

10 Thomas Hinds Tobacconists
MAP D3 ▪ 8 Cumberland St

A smoker's paradise, this shop has a walk-in humidor with a full range of Cuban and Latin American cigars, and two lounges in which to enjoy them. Stellar selection of tobaccos, cigarettes, and accessories.

See map on pp74–5 ←

West Queen West Shops

1 C Squared
MAP G4 ▪ 693 Queen St W (just west of Bathurst)

The impressive selection of Campers, Marc, and hand-crafted Cydwoqs attracts those looking for funky footwear.

2 Morba
MAP G4 ▪ 665 Queen St W (just west of Bathurst)

Mid-century modern emporium with loads of second-hand teak, light fixtures, and Finnish glass, plus 1950s-inspired bits-and-bobs for the kitchen and office.

 Second-hand typewriter, Morba

3 Anthropologie
MAP B4 ▪ 761 Queen St W

This store's setting – in a converted former church with stained-glass windows – is as beautiful as the clothes, shoes, accessories, and home furnishings it sells.

4 Heel Boy
MAP B4 ▪ 773 Queen St W

This is a hip shoe boutique for men and women. Prices ($100 to $400-plus) are good, and the quality and selection are excellent. They stock everything – from sandals to espadrilles to lace-up booties.

5 Drake General Store
MAP A4 ▪ 1144 Queen St W (at Beaconsfield Ave)

Attached to The Drake's Hotel, this Canadiana shop is a great place to shop for gifts. There are branches at Yonge and Eglinton and in the Bay at Yonge and Queen.

6 Type Books
MAP B4 ▪ 883 Queen St W (across from Trinity Bellwoods Park)

A cozy independent with a great range of fiction and design titles and an inspired children's section.

7 The Paper Place
MAP B4 ▪ 887 Queen St W

This Japanese-inspired store stocks a gorgeous selection of Chiyogami silk-screened paper, as well as ribbon, cards, and wrapping paper.

8 Fred Perry
MAP A4 ▪ 964 Queen St W

Mod-style threads from this UK designer chain include Laurel-insignia collared tees, trainers, and classic leather sports bags.

9 Lavish & Squalor
MAP J4 ▪ 253 Queen St W

Known for soy wax candles in amber jars, this hip shop and café stocks various Canadian treasures, from raw denim apparel to home accessories.

10 Coal Miner's Daughter
MAP B4 ▪ 744 Queen St W (at Niagara St)

There are pretty, alternative designs and a handmade ethos at this inde-pendent boutique. They sell local and Swedish jewelry and vintage shoes.

Fashions at Coal Miner's Daughter

Bars and Pubs

The Oxley, a stylish gastro pub

1 The Oxley
MAP C3 ■ 121 Yorkville Ave
■ 647 348 1300

In a neighborhood packed with wine bars, the Oxley is a comfortable gastro pub offering down-to-earth grub and a great range of beers.

2 The Queen and Beaver
MAP L2 ■ 35 Elm St ■ 647 347 2712

This quirky take on an English pub puts an equally tasty twist on its fare – try the unusual stilton ice cream.

3 Dog and Bear
MAP A4 ■ 1100 Queen St W
■ 647 352 8601

A friendly pub hung with Union Jacks and sporting dark red flocked wallpaper. Sports-mad with numerous screens, and DJs on weekends.

4 The Roof Lounge
MAP C2 ■ 4 Avenue Rd
■ 416 924 5471

Snag a seat on the 18th-floor terrace for the view, or savor the warm atmosphere inside the Roof Lounge *(see p59)*.

5 Lula Lounge
MAP A4 ■ 1585 Dundas St W
■ 416 588 0307 ■ Adm

Salsa gets the hips swaying, as rum cocktails loosen you up at this *(see p58)* Little Portugal hotspot.

6 Cameron House
MAP H3 ■ 408 Queen St W
■ 416 703 0811 ■ Adm (for backroom shows)

Hang out with the locals and catch great local roots, folk, and indie bands in this ornate yet casual bar *(see p59)*. The changing murals on the facade are a local landmark.

7 180 Panorama
MAP D3 ■ 55 Bloor St W
■ 416 967 0000 ■ Adm

Not for acrophobics, this bar's patios, on the 51st floor of the Manulife Centre, are the city's highest.

8 d|bar
MAP D3 ■ 60 Yorkville Ave
■ 416 963 6010

Linger over a cocktail or glass of chardonnay in this chic bar *(see p58)*, then do some people-watching.

Cozy interior of The Drake Lounge

9 The Drake Lounge
MAP A4 ■ 1150 Queen St W
■ 416 531 5042

Recline on a comfy sofa beside the fireplace while taking in the scene, including the Raw Bar peddling its oysters. Afterwards, check out the live music or art happening downstairs in the underground bar.

10 The Paddock
MAP G4 ■ 178 Bathurst St
■ 416 504 9997

Although red leather banquettes prompt a twinge of 1950s nostalgia, this bar is rooted in the 21st century.

See map on pp74–5

International Eats

1 Bahn Mi Boys
MAP L2 ■ 399 Yonge St
■ 416 977 0303 ■ $

Traditional Vietnamese *bahn mi* baguettes (stuffed with grilled pork, sausage or paté, grated veg and cilantro) are served with pulled pork or squid. Try the kimchi fries.

2 Boulevard Café
MAP C3 ■ 161 Harbord St
■ 416 961 7676 ■ $

The city's oldest Peruvian restaurant offers grilled meats and seafood. Tapas are served in the upstairs lounge and on the patio in summer.

3 Mother's Dumplings
MAP H2 ■ 421 Spadina Ave
■ 416 217 2008 ■ $

This traditional shop excels at juicy pork buns and creative dumpling selections such as pork and radish.

4 Banjara Indian Cuisine
MAP B3 ■ 796 Bloor St W
■ 416 963 9360 ■ $$

An unfussy, diner-like interior belies the fine Indian cooking for which Banjara has become famous.

An authentic setting at Julie's Cuban

5 Julie's Cuban
MAP A4 ■ 202 Dovercourt Rd
■ 416 532 7397 ■ $

Checkered table cloths, vintage salt and pepper shakers, a warm welcome, and good, earthy Cuban food.

Italian fare, Café Diplomatico

6 Café Diplomatico
MAP B3 ■ 594 College St
■ 416 534 4637 ■ $

The patio is the place to be at this Little Italy institution. Pizza, pasta, and panzerotti are on the menu, but it's also popular for people-watching.

7 Korea House
MAP B3 ■ 666 Bloor St W
■ 416 536 8666 ■ $

This family-run restaurant cooks up traditional Korean fare. Try the Korean rice wines or *soju*, distilled liquors flavored with fruit or flowers.

8 El Trompo
MAP H2 ■ 277 Augusta Ave
■ 416 260 0097 ■ $

A fun, lively Mexican place right in the heart of Kensington Market. If you're lucky you'll snag a seat on the patio to take in the streetlife.

9 Sashimi Island
MAP B3 ■ 635 College St
■ 416 535 1888 ■ $

One of many all-you-can-eat sushi joints. Refined Japanese dining it is not, but if you are just after *maki* rolls, then this will hit the spot.

10 Churrasqueira do Sardinha
MAP B3 ■ 707 College St ■ 416 531 1120 ■ $

Portuguese rotisserie chicken is a local tradition. This spotless takeout and eat-in spot is a favorite, known for its spicy sauce ribs.

→ *See map on pp74–5*

Restaurants and Cafés

 Aunties and Uncles
MAP B3 ■ 74 Lippincott S
■ 416 324 1375 ■ Closed D ■ $

A quirky, retro-style diner that offers comfort food favorites such as Canadian cheddar grilled cheese and cinnamon french toast.

2 Fresh
MAP C4 ■ 326 Bloor St W
■ 416 599 4442 ■ $$

A vegetarian eatery providing a filling meal and loads of choice. Noodle bowls and vitamin-packed juices suit all who need a healthy pick-up. Branches at Queen West, Crawford, Richmond, and Spadina.

3 Noce
MAP B4 ■ 875 Queen St W
■ 416 504 3463 ■ Closed Mon & L ■ $$

Noce serves house-made pasta, pizzas, meat, and seafood, and all of its dishes incorporate a creative, wood-fired element.

4 ALO
MAP H4 ■ 163 Spadina Ave ■ 416 260 2222 ■ Closed Sun, Mon & L ■ $$$

ALO serves a nine-course French tasting menu, called one of Toronto's "most remarkable" dining experiences. For a mid-priced meal, opt to sit at the bar.

5 Buca Yorkville
MAP C3 ■ 53 Scollard St
■ 416 962 2822 ■ $$$

A seafood-oriented Italian restaurant known not just for the freshness and variety of its fish dishes but also for the creative pastas and pizzas.

Stylish interiors of Buca Yorkville

PRICE CATEGORIES

Price categories include a three-course meal for one, half a bottle of wine, and all unavoidable extra charges including tax.

$ under $50 $$ $50–120 $$$ over $120

6 La Palette
MAP H2 ■ 492 Queen St W
■ 416 929 4900 ■ $$$

This bohemian space tempts with good-value French food, and takes its pedigree to heart, offering horse tenderloin to adventurous diners.

7 Opus
MAP C3 ■ 37 Prince Arthur Ave
■ 416 921 3105 ■ Closed L ■ $$$

This refined dining room has one of the best wine lists in the city. Tuna tartare with caviar, and the roasted meats get top marks.

8 Mildred's Temple Kitchen
MAP A5 ■ 85 Hanna Ave ■ 416 588 5695 ■ Closed Sun–Tue D ■ $$

Pioneers of the brunch trend, Mildred's is still going strong 20 years later. Expect classic dishes featuring seasonal, regional ingredients.

9 Dark Horse Espresso Bar
MAP H3 ■ 215 Spadina Ave
■ 416 979 1200 ■ $

Its personal feel and great-quality coffee make the Dark Horse the ideal spot for a pick-me-up.

10 Lai Wah Heen
MAP K3 ■ 108 Chestnut St
■ 416 977 9899 ■ $$

Translating to "luxurious meeting place," this elegant eatery has been serving first-rate dim sum since 1995.

TOP 10 East

This region of contrasts has some of the city's grandest old mansions on the stately Jarvis and Sherbourne streets. Cabbagetown, originally a working-class Irish immigrant neighborhood with Victorian cottages and rowhouses, has now been transformed into an upscale district of urban professionals. The area has many historic sights as well as a vibrant streetlife thanks to the lively LGBT+ oriented village along Church Street, the fresh-food destination of St. Lawrence Market, and the Greek and Macedonian enclave of the Danforth. To the south, a complex of Victorian buildings has been converted into the Distillery Historic District, a popular shopping and entertainment destination.

Mackenzie House exhibit

EAST

1 Top 10 Sights
see pp87–9

1 Restaurants
see p93

1 St. Lawrence Market
see p90

1 Bars and Pubs
see p92

1 Shops
see p91

Clock at Distillery Historic District

1 Distillery Historic District

This Victorian industrial district (see pp26–7) is now one of the city's most interesting and picturesque. Pedestrian-only cobblestone streets lead past old warehouses and historic factories stunningly preserved and renovated to house galleries, restaurants, performance venues, and specialty shops.

2 Cabbagetown
MAP E3–E4

One of Toronto's oldest subdivisions, dating to the 1840s, this district was a working-class community well into the 1970s. Many of the cottages and Victorian homes have since been renovated, and it is now an upscale residential enclave that makes for a pleasant stroll. On the east side is Riverdale Park and its delightful Riverdale Farm (see p51). Across the street, set within the grounds of the Necropolis Cemetery, is an 1872 chapel, a Gothic Revival treasure. At the north end of Cabbagetown, St. James Cemetery, Toronto's oldest, has many beautiful crypts.

Necropolis Cemetery, Cabbagetown

3 Mackenzie House
MAP L3 ▪ 82 Bond St ▪ 416 392 6915 ▪ Open Jan–Apr: noon–5pm Sat & Sun; May–early Sep: noon–5pm Tue–Sun; Sep–Dec: noon–4pm Tue–Fri, noon–5pm Sat & Sun ▪ Adm

This Greek Revival rowhouse, built in 1858, was the home of Toronto's first mayor, William Lyon Mackenzie. Now a period museum, it features a re-created print shop and a gallery with changing exhibitions.

A colorful building representative of the vibrant Church Street scene

(4) Church Street
MAP L1–L2

The hub of Toronto's LGBT+ oriented Village, Church Street from Carleton Street to north of Wellesley Street, is vibrant day and night. Restaurants and bars cater to an out crowd, and specialty shops abound. Pick up a copy of the free daily newspaper *Xtra!* for listings of everything the village has to offer.

(5) St. Lawrence Market
MAP M5 ■ 92–5 Front St E

Considered one of the world's great markets, the St. Lawrence complex *(see p90)* consists of South Market and North Market (currently being redeveloped). The 120-plus vendors sell great fresh food products, and there is also an antiques market.

(6) Allan Gardens
MAP M2

This large park embodies the contradictions of the downtown eastside. It is both grand and gritty. Best explored during the day, the gardens, which first opened in 1860, contain a delightful glass-and-metal conservatory complex consisting of six greenhouses built in 1910, each with a different climate zone. Inside, the exuberant displays of seasonal and permanent greenery and flowers delight the senses.

(7) Todmorden Mills Heritage Site
MAP F2 ■ 67 Pottery Rd ■ Historic Buildings: open Jan–May & Sep–Dec: noon–4pm Wed–Fri (until 4:30pm Sat & Sun); Jun–Aug: 10am–4:30pm Tue–Fri, noon–5pm Sat & Sun ■ Adm ■ Grounds: open daily

This collection of late 18th-century buildings imparts the feel of a historic village, and fine examples of the original industrial architecture pepper the site. Two of the houses – the 1797 Terry Cottage and 1800s Helliwell House – have been restored with period furnishings. The Paper Mill Gallery and Theatre stages performances and art shows. A wild flower preserve bursts with trilliums in spring, and trails offer lots of wildlife-spotting opportunities.

DON RIVER

The Don is one of the defining natural features of Toronto. Flowing east of downtown into Lake Ontario, the steep river valley cuts a swath through the city. While industrial use of the river has degraded the water, naturalization projects have started the long process of restoring the valley to ecological health. The ribbon of linked green spaces following the Don's course means that you can hike and cycle right through the center of the city.

8 The Danforth
MAP F3

Linked to downtown by the 1918 Prince Edward Viaduct, which spans the Don River Valley, the Danforth has been home to thriving Greek and Macedonian communities since the 1950s. In early August, the weeklong Taste of the Danforth street festival is a smorgasbord of tasty treats and entertainment.

9 Toronto's First Post Office
MAP M4 ▪ 260 Adelaide St E ▪ 416 865 1833 ▪ Open 9am–5:30pm Mon–Fri, 10am–4pm Sat, noon–4pm Sun ▪ Adm (by donation)

This working post office and museum opened in 1833 and is the only surviving example of a British-era post office in Canada. Here, you can write a letter with a quill pen and have it stamped with a distinctive cancellation mark: "York-Toronto 1833." There is also a topographic model of 1830s Toronto, period furniture, and 19th-century reproduction ink wells and sealing wax.

Toronto's First Post Office

10 Evergreen Brick Works
MAP E2 ▪ 550 Bayview Ave

The smokestack is just one of the historic features that remain at this once-thriving industrial complex (see p47), which opened in 1889 to produce bricks using clay found on site. The quarry has been returned to nature as a park with ponds and meadows, and the industrial buildings redeveloped as a sustainable development showcase. There is also a restaurant and adventure playground.

A CABBAGETOWN STROLL

▶ MORNING

Begin your day at **Jet Fuel** (519 Parliament Street) with a strong espresso. After your caffeine jolt, turn right and walk north to Wellesley Street, then turn right again and walk east to take in the charming Victorian architecture. Note the strange animal and face carvings on No. 314. Explore the lanes running north, including Wellesley Cottages, a courtyard with seven gabled cottages tucked behind the street. As you come to the end of Wellesley, spend a few moments wandering through Wellesley Park, enjoying the view across the Don Valley.

Backtrack to Wellesley and turn left onto Sumach Street; its charming houses are classic **Cabbagetown** (see p87). Note Second Empire-style Nos. 420–22, built in 1886, and the English cottage style of Nos 404–08. Turn left at Winchester Street; Necropolis Cemetery will be on the left. Peek into the chapel to admire the stained glass.

AFTERNOON

For lunch, head back along Winchester Street to Parliament Street, where you'll find **Peartree Restaurant** (No. 507). After lunch, meander through the compact streets – Metcalfe, Salisbury, and Sackville – before walking east to Riverdale Park and its **Riverdale Farm** (see p51). Cute **Winchester Café** (161 Winchester Street), dispensing refreshments through a side window, is situated just across the street from the park's northwest corner.

See map on pp86–7

St. Lawrence Market

Undercover market stalls selling fresh food items, St. Lawrence Market

1 St. Lawrence Market South

Open 8am–6pm Tue–Thu, 8am–7pm Fri & 5am–5pm Sat

Opened in 1845 as Toronto's second City Hall, this building now houses a thriving public market selling some of the freshest produce.

2 St. Lawrence Market North

Open 5am–early afternoon Sat

North Market is being redeveloped. The vendors are temporarily operating from a block south at 125 Esplanade.

3 European Delight

This Ukrainian mainstay in South Market's lower level serves up home-made favorites – cabbage rolls, *perogies* (dumplings) – for takeout; you can also buy them frozen.

4 Sunday Antique Market

From 5am on Sunday, vendors offer piles of knick-knacks as well as more serious pieces such as military collectibles and mid-century design classics (at 125 Esplanade while the North Market is being refurbished).

5 Montreal Bagels

Locals love St. Urbain Bakery's dense, chewy buns (South Market). Their bagel-cooking method – which involves boiling then baking them in a wood-fired oven – hails from the French-Canadian city of Montreal.

6 Alex Farm Products

A cheese-lover's paradise, in South Market, this stall sells every kind of cheese, from French cantal to the most pungent of blues. Good raw-milk cheese selection.

7 Buskers and Craft-Sellers

Lively street action is part of the charm of market Saturdays, as buskers entertain and craftspeople ply their wares outside the south buildings during warmer months.

8 Peameal Bacon Sandwiches

Quintessentially Canadian, and perfect to fuel up for the day, the kaiser buns at South Market's Carousel Bakery are stuffed with salty, peameal-encrusted pork.

9 Market Gallery

Open 10am–4pm Tue–Fri, 9am–4pm Sat ■ Adm to some exhibits

Artifacts and historical photographs of the city are exhibited in themed shows in the old council chamber on the second floor of South Market.

10 Buster's Sea Cove

416 369 9048 ■ Open Tue–Sat

A delightful spot to enjoy Boston's blue fish and chips plate and lobster roll, Buster's Sea Cove also offers hearty portions of battered golden fish with curly fries.

Shops

 Negash & Dessa
MAP F3 ■ 161 Danforth Ave
■ 416 462 9306

This shop sells an excellent range of accessories including a sophisticated range of leather goods, and sleek silver jewelry too.

 The Big Carrot
MAP F3 ■ Carrot Common Complex, 348 Danforth Ave ■ 416 466 2129

Lovers of organic foods and natural body care will love this large and well-stocked grocery store, where they can recharge by sampling the delicious prepared foods and organic juices on offer here.

③ Soma Chocolate
MAP E5 ■ 32 Tank House Lane ■ 416 815 7662

A must-visit for the chocolate cognoscenti. Sample the confections or try a cup of steaming Mayan hot chocolate, redolent with spices.

Gadabout, located in Leslieville

④ Gadabout
MAP F4 ■ 1300 Queen St E ■ 416 463 1254

Get lost in time at this tiny vintage store. Oddments from around the globe are packed into display cases, and there are plenty of vintage finds.

⑤ Bergo Designs
MAP E5 ■ 28 Tank House Lane ■ 416 861 1821

In the Distillery Historic District, this boutique calls itself a gallery of design. Cutting-edge items, from jewelry to furniture to kitchen gadgets, could double as artworks, making them perfect gifts.

⑥ John Fluevog
MAP E5 ■ 4 Trinity St ■ 416 583 1970

Famous cobbler Fluevog, who hails from Vancouver and has been making his solid, unusual shoes for years, now sells his footwear in the vibrant Distillery Historic District's Boiler House Complex.

⑦ Artsmarket
MAP F4 ■ 1114 Queen St E ■ 416 546 8464

Artists, craftspeople and vintage collectors, display their vastly differing wares in small, close-knit spaces. Good fun on a lively Leslieville block.

⑧ Ethel
MAP E4 ■ 327 Queen St E ■ 416 778 6608

Elegant teak dining tables, glass and acrylic coffee tables, and other nifty pieces from the 1960s and 1970s, at reasonable prices.

⑨ Kristapsons
MAP F4 ■ 1095 Queen St E ■ 416 466 5152

Pacific salmon, cold-smoked on the premises using a secret recipe, is all you'll find in this store – but what a find. Those in the know claim it ranks among the world's best.

⑩ Henry's
MAP L4 ■ 119 Church St ■ 416 868 0872

Everything a photographer needs, from the latest digital cameras to vintage Leica lenses, and necessities such as film, batteries, photo paper, and a quality developing service.

See map on pp86–7➜

Bars and Pubs

 Betty's
MAP M4 ■ 240 King St E
■ 416 368 1300

This pub offers beers on tap, tasty food such Montreal smoked meat on rye, billiard tables, and a patio.

 Mill Street Brew Pub
MAP E5 ■ 21 Tank House Lane ■ 416 681 0338

Sample the 13 brews on tap while gazing on the vats of beer fermenting in the glass-walled brewery.

③ **Imperial Pub Tavern**
MAP L3 ■ 54 Dundas St E
■ 416 977 4667

Customers treasure the circular bar and jukeboxes playing old jazz hits in this no-frills place.

 Stout Irish Pub
MAP E4 ■ 221 Carlton St
■ 647 344 7676

With a changing beer menu, creative pub food, and fun trivia nights, this tavern draws a devoted clientele.

⑤ **Consort Bar**
MAP L4 ■ 37 King St E
■ 416 863 3131

Relish the great whiskeys and masterfully mixed cocktails in this dignified bar at the Omni King Edward Hotel *(see p117)*.

The stately Consort Bar

⑥ **Dora Keogh**
MAP F3 ■ 141 Danforth Ave
■ 416 778 1804

A reconstructed 1890s Irish pub, with dark-wood benches, stools, and little tables. Good selection of beers and whiskeys. Live music most nights.

Irish music session, Ceílí Cottage

⑦ **Ceílí Cottage**
MAP F4 ■ 1301 Queen St E
■ 416 406 1301

Snug, rustic Irish bar with excellent food and good hand-pulled beer (no bottles), and traditional Irish music on Tuesday nights.

⑧ **C'est What?**
MAP L5 ■ 67 Front St E
■ 416 867 9499

A casual spot with 35 microbrews on tap, some, such as the hemp, rye, and coffee brews, produced exclusively for the pub. Live music some nights and Sunday afternoons.

⑨ **Pravda Vodka House**
MAP L4 ■ 44 Wellington St E
■ 416 366 0303

Enjoy Russian-inspired food and endless vodka at this restaurant *(see p58)* with Soviet-themed decor.

⑩ **BeerBistro**
MAP L4 ■ 18 King St E
■ 416 861 9872

Beer is taken seriously here with an enormous selection. Many menu items incorporate beers too.

Restaurants

PRICE CATEGORIES

Price categories include a three-course meal for one, half a bottle of wine, and all unavoidable extra charges including tax.

$ under $50 $$ $50–120 $$$ over $120

 Lady Marmalade
MAP F4 ■ 898 Queen St E
■ 647 351 7645 ■ Closed D ■ $

Serving eggs Benedict and Mexican dishes with organic, seasonal produce, this friendly, locals' spot offers all-day breakfast and lunch.

2 Pizza Libretto
MAP F3 ■ 550 Danforth Ave
■ 416 466 0400 ■ $

This lively spot serves up the most authentic Neapolitan pizzas in town. Reserve ahead for a table or perch at the window.

3 Mezes
MAP F3 ■ 456
Danforth Ave ■ 416
361 5634 ■ $

This Greektown favorite encourages sharing – appropriate since Mezes means "small plates." Try the steamed mussels, spicy feta as well as *saganaki* – the cheese dish that arrives at the table flambéed.

 Batifole
MAP F4 ■ 744 Gerrard St E ■ 416
462 9965 ■ Closed Sun, Mon & L ■ $$

Devoted Francophiles flock to this unpretentious restaurant on the outer edge of Chinatown East for classics such as *cassoulet* and *soupe de poissons*.

5 Sauvignon Bistro
MAP B2 ■ 1862 Queen St E
■ 416 686 1998 ■ Closed L ■ $$

This cozy spot is a haunt for locals of the Beach. Relax on the sidewalk patio and enjoy steak frites, duck confit or other bistro-style dishes.

 Allen's
MAP F3 ■ 143 Danforth Ave
■ 416 463 3086 ■ $$

Grab a wooden booth at the front of this pub-restaurant or eat out on one of the best patios in the city.

7 Lake Inez
MAP B2 ■ 1471 Gerrard St E
■ 416 792 1590 ■ Closed Mon,
Tue & L ■ $$

Filipino- and Asian-inspired cuisine is paired with craft beer at Lake Inez. Do not miss the grilled pork chops.

8 El Catrin
MAP E5 ■ 18 Tank House Lane
■ 416 203 2121 ■ $$

Set in the Distillery Historic District, this huge Mexican restaurant has Day of the Dead-themed decor.

Hand-painted wall mural, El Catrin

9 Udupi Palace
MAP B2 ■ 1460 Gerrard St E
■ 416 405 8189 ■ $

Locals flock to this South Indian vegetarian spot for delicious snacks and stuffed *dosas*. Try the *thali* to taste a mix of exciting flavors.

10 Gio Rana's Really, Really Nice Restaurant
MAP B4 ■ 1220 Queen St E ■ 416
469 5225 ■ Closed Sun & L ■ $$

This unconventionally named and decorated restaurant is housed in a former bank and specializes in great-value southern Italian fare.

See map on pp86–7

TOP 10 Greater Toronto

Artifact from Colborne Lodge

The area surrounding the city proper has expanded rapidly in the last few decades, with suburban bedroom communities popping up around the urban fringe and engulfing fertile farmland. Although highway development ensures access to the many sites outside the city, roads can be extremely crowded at rush hour. Many parks and natural areas lie just outside the city, along with spacious beaches. One of Toronto's most popular sights, the Ontario Science Centre, is a delightful place to spend a day, as is, for family thrills, Canada's Wonderland. Historic attractions, such as Black Creek Pioneer Village, where costumed guides demonstrate pioneer life, offer a glimpse into 19th-century country life. Art lovers are drawn to the McMichael Canadian Art Collection in charming Kleinburg.

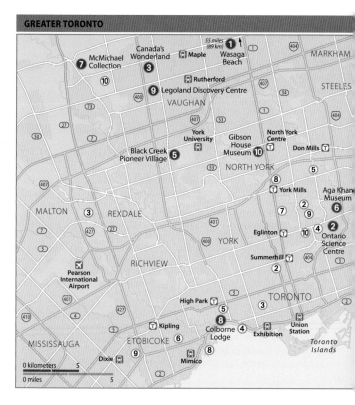

GREATER TORONTO

1 Wasaga Beach
MAP B1

In summer, residents of the city flock to the world's longest freshwater beach, Wasaga. Gold sands offset pristine blue waters on the Nottawasaga Bay at the end of the Georgian Bay, which is suitable for swimming. There are watersport rentals as well as many trails for cycling and hiking. Annually, it draws millions of visitors.

2 Ontario Science Centre
MAP B1 ■ 770 Don Mills Rd ■ 416 696 1000 ■ Open 10am–4pm Mon–Fri (until 8pm Sat, 5pm Sun)

Exhibits here are interactive and geared toward youngsters. Eleven themed areas cover a diverse range of topics, including Earth's ecosystems, space, sport, energy, communication, and the human body.

Roller coaster, Canada's Wonderland

3 Canada's Wonderland
MAP A1 ■ 9580 Jane St, Vaughan ■ 905 832 8131 ■ Open mid-Jun–Aug: 10am–10pm daily; Sep: 10am–8pm Sat & Sun; Oct: 10am–5pm Sat & Sun (opening hours may vary) ■ Adm ■ www.canadaswonderland.com

This theme park north of Toronto draws crowds with over 200 attractions, 69 rides, and a water park. Thrills abound, the biggest pleasers being the roller coasters.

4 The Beach
MAP B2

Taking full advantage of its lakeside setting, The Beach feels more like a small resort town. In summer, crowds throng to the white-sand beaches, stroll the boardwalk, picnic in Kew Gardens, and go shopping along Queen Street. The area is at its busiest in late July, during the Beaches International Jazz Festival (see p63).

A performance at the Jazz Festival

5 Black Creek Pioneer Village

MAP A1 ■ 1000 Murray Ross Pkwy ■ 416 736 1733 ■ Open May–Jun: 9:30am–4pm Mon–Fri, 11am–5pm Sat & Sun; Jul–Labour Day: 10am–5pm Mon–Fri, 11am–5pm Sat & Sun; Labour Day–Dec 25: 9:30am–4pm Mon–Fri, 11am–4:30pm Sat & Sun ■ Adm

For an authentic taste of early settler life in Canada, visit this re-creation of a 19th-century rural Ontario community. Among the dozens of buildings are a school, a church, village shops, houses, and barns. The grounds include an orchard, millpond, restored gardens, and grazing livestock. Costumed staff demonstrate pioneer crafts and carry out tasks such as tinsmithing and milling flour.

6 Aga Khan Museum

MAP B2 ■ 77 Wynford Dr ■ Open 10am–6pm Tue–Sun (until 8pm Thu) ■ Adm ■ www.agakhan museum.org

Housed in a distinctive building by Japanese architect Fumihiko Maki, the museum (see p43) holds Islamic treasures, including ceramics, textiles, scientific texts, and musical instruments, as well as undiscovered masterpieces such as delicately painted folios from *Shahnameh* or Book of Kings (Iran, 16th century). The collection high-lights the cultural diversity of Muslim society, from Spain, through Africa and the Middle East, to China.

> **R. C. HARRIS FILTRATION PLANT**
>
> Built in the late 1930s, this filtration plant has been dubbed the "palace of purification." Perched atop a gentle hill, this Art Deco structure holds the machines that treat the city's drinking water, which is pumped into the facility from a pipe that begins about 1.5 miles (2 km) offshore, in Lake Ontario. Nearly 200 million gallons (757 million litres) of water are processed daily, supplying about half of Toronto's needs.

7 McMichael Canadian Art Collection

MAP A1 ■ 10365 Islington Ave, Kleinburg, 18 miles (30 km) North of Toronto ■ 905 893 1121 ■ Open May–Oct: 10am–5pm daily; Nov–Apr: 10am–4pm Tue–Sun ■ Adm

McMichael Canadian Art Collection

This outstanding gallery features a stellar display of works by the seminal Group of Seven painters, their contemporaries such as Tom Thomson and Emily Carr, and the artists they inspired. There's also an impressive collection of works by First Nations and Inuit artists.

8 Colborne Lodge

MAP A2 ■ Colborne Lodge Dr ■ 416 392 6916 ■ Open Jan, Feb & Apr: noon–4pm Sat & Sun; Mar: noon–4pm Thu–Sun; May–Aug: noon–5pm Tue–Sun; Sep: noon–5pm Sat & Sun; Oct–Dec: noon–4pm Tue–Sun ■ Adm

This 1837 house was the residence of land surveyor John Howard and his wife, Jemima. Howard deeded

The noteworthy exterior of the Aga Khan Museum

his estate to the city, thereby forming the basis for High Park *(see p98)*. Located at the south end of the park, the Regency-style house, with its gorgeous circular verandah, has been fully restored and holds many of the Howards' original belongings, including John Howard's original watercolors of early Toronto scenes. Costumed guides lead tours. Don't miss the garden, planted with kitchen herbs and flowers.

Kids at the Legoland Discovery Centre

9 Legoland Discovery Centre

MAP A1 ■ 1 Bass Pro Mills Dr, Vaughan ■ 1 855 356 2150 ■ Open 10am–7:30pm Mon–Thu, 10am–8pm Fri & Sat, 11am–7pm Sun (last admittance 2 hours before closing) ■ Adm

Little builders aged 3 to 10 will love this indoor complex *(see p53)* packed with all things LEGO®, including a Miniland of landmarks and a LEGO® car speed test track. Adults must be accompanied by a child to be admitted.

10 Gibson House Museum

MAP A1 ■ 5172 Yonge St ■ 416 395 7432 ■ Open 1–5pm Wed–Sun, 1–8pm Thu (Jul & Aug: from 11am) ■ Guided tours available ■ Adm

This elegant Georgian farmhouse was built in 1851. The original owner, David Gibson, was a leader of the Upper Canada Rebellion in 1837 – he was forced to flee to the US when the uprising failed. Following his pardon, Gibson returned and built this home for his family.

A DAY AT THE BEACH

▶ MORNING

Start off your day with a great breakfast at the **Sunset Grill** *(see p51)* – the waffles are a local favorite. Cross the street and meander toward the lake through **Kew Gardens** *(see p95)*, noting the rounded windows of the 1902 Kew Williams Cottage at the park's south end. Reaching the boardwalk, turn right and follow it to the end, a 15-minute stroll. Look out for the paved path on the right; take it into **Ashbridges Bay Park** *(see p47)*, where you can stroll along the waterfront, watching sailboats moor and enjoying excellent views across the city from the west side. For lunch, retrace your steps to Kew Gardens, then up to Queen Street, for a famously good burger at **Hero Certified Burgers** *(No. 2018)*. Eat in or take out and sit in Kew Gardens across the street.

AFTERNOON

Spend your afternoon browsing the shops on Queen Street E, maybe picking up a treat at **The Nutty Chocolatier** *(No. 2179)* to enjoy while taking a break at the serene sunken rock garden – **Ivan Forrest Gardens** – at Queen Street E and Glen Manor Drive. When shopped out, snag a seat on **Outrigger's** patio *(No. 2232)* and relax with a drink. If you're up for more walking, continue for another 10 minutes east to the **R. C. Harris Filtration Plant** *(see p96)* to stroll the grounds of this Art Deco gem and admire the view of the **Scarborough Bluffs** *(see p98)* and Lake Ontario.

See map on pp94–5

Green Spaces

Birdlife, Rouge Urban Park

1 Rouge National Urban Park
MAP B1 ▪ www.rouge park.com

Following the course of the Rouge River, this is one of North America's largest urban parks (see p47). It contains the wildest natural area in the city.

2 Toronto Botanical Garden
MAP B1 ▪ 777 Lawrence Ave E ▪ 416 397 1340

Magnificent floral displays feature in this park by the Wilket Creek ravine.

3 Humber Arboretum
MAP A2 ▪ 205 Humber College Blvd

Set near the West Humber River, this nature center has self-guided trails through woodlands and meadows, and exhibits on plants and wildlife.

4 Martin Goodman Trail
MAP A2–B2

Hugging the shore of Lake Ontario, the 35-mile (56-km) multiuse trail connects the waterfront parks.

5 High Park
MAP A2 ▪ 1873 Bloor St W

Toronto's largest downtown park (see p46) has long trails, along with play areas, tennis courts, a small zoo, and a snack bar and restaurant.

High Park, a lovely green space

6 Bluffer's Park
MAP B2 ▪ Brimley Rd, south end

Dramatic sandstone cliffs rise 350 ft (107 m) above Lake Ontario, providing a spectacular backdrop to this east-end park with a marina.

7 Guildwood Park
MAP B1 ▪ 201 Guildwood Pkwy

Enjoy gardens and naturalized areas full of woodland wild flowers at this Scarborough Bluff park. Intriguing architectural artifacts saved from demolished buildings are spread throughout the grounds.

8 Humber Bay Butterfly Habitat
MAP A2 ▪ Humber Bay Park Rd E

Flowers and plants attract butterflies at this lakeshore park with a great view of the city's skyline. A demonstration garden highlights flowers for home gardens that attract butterflies.

9 Sunnybrook Park
MAP B1 ▪ Enter west of Leslie St via Wilket Creek Park

Encompassing shady Burke Ravine, this park provides respite from the summer heat. There are interpretive nature trails, riding stables, sports fields, picnic tables, and a café.

10 Kortright Center
MAP A1 ▪ 9550 Pine Valley Dr, Woodbridge ▪ 905 832 2289 ▪ Adm

This conservation area has hands-on activities and guided nature walks – nighttime "owl prowls" are popular. Miles of trails lead through forests, meadows, and river valleylands.

Restaurants

 Ho Ho BBQ
MAP B1 ▪ 3833 Midland Ave
▪ 416 321 9818 ▪ $

The team at Ho Ho's barbecues pork and duck better than anyone else in Chinatown. The delicious crispy skin complements the tender meat that is served in paper cartons.

② **Scaramouche**
MAP C2 ▪ 1 Benvenuto Pl
▪ 416 961 8011 ▪ Closed Sun & L ▪ $$

The Pasta Bar at this venue is a city institution, and it is less pricey than the elegant main room, which has been serving up inventive cuisine for decades. Fabulous view of the city.

③ **Chiado**
MAP A3 ▪ 864 College St
▪ 416 538 1910 ▪ $$$

Excellent fresh seafood and hearty Portuguese meat dishes are served in an old-world, upscale dining room. Extensive Portuguese wine list.

④ **Adamson Barbecue**
MAP B1 ▪ 176 Wicksteed Ave
▪ 647 559 2080 ▪ Closed Mon ▪ $$

Wood-smoked brisket, ribs, and turkey breast are offered here. It is open from lunch until the meat is sold out.

⑤ **Katsura**
MAP B1 ▪ Westin Prince Hotel,
900 York Mills Rd ▪ 416 444 2511
▪ Closed Sat & Sun L ▪ $$

Japanese specialties such as sushi, *sashimi*, *tempura*, and grilled fish are served at the sushi bar, around *teppan* tables in the dining room, or in private *tatami* rooms.

⑥ **Sushi Kaji**
MAP A2 ▪ 860 The Queensway
▪ 416 252 2166 ▪ Closed Mon, Tue & L
▪ $$$

Set-menu options, including the deluxe, chef's choice *omakase* menu, present course after course of wonderful, complex Japanese creations balanced with simple, incredibly fresh *sashimi* and sushi.

PRICE CATEGORIES

Price categories include a three-course meal for one, half a bottle of wine, and all unavoidable extra charges including tax.

$ under $50 $$ $50–$120 $$$ over $120

⑦ **STACK**
MAP B1 ▪ 3265 Yonge St
▪ 647 346 1416 ▪ $$

Large restaurant offering southern barbecue, burgers, and doughnuts. The secret to its popularity is the perfect execution of a simple concept.

⑧ **Auberge du Pommier**
MAP B1 ▪ 4150 Yonge St ▪ 416
222 2220 ▪ Closed Sun & Mon ▪ $$$

Classic French cooking with a modern twist. There are two intimate rooms, a bar, and a small patio. In winter, ask to sit by the fireplace.

Foie gras, Auberge du Pommier

⑨ **Via Allegro**
MAP A2 ▪ 1750 The Queensway
▪ 416 622 6677 ▪ $$

Authentic Italian food such as pasta, seafood, and wood-fired oven pizzas are on offer. The award-winning wine cellar, with over 5,000 selections, is an oenophile magnet.

⑩ **Indian Street Food**
MAP B2 ▪ 1701 Bayview Ave
▪ 416 322 3270 ▪ $$

This bright and lively East York spot offers a modern slant on the meals found at Indian train stations. Try dishes such as charcoal-grilled prawns or chicken tikka. The no-tipping policy is a bonus.

See map on pp94–5

Top10 Beyond Toronto

Within easy driving distance of Toronto are many delightful communities. North of the city, Honey Harbour and Gravenhurst are the gateways to cottage country, with beautiful lakes and forests, while Collingwood offers skiing in winter and summer fun on Georgian Bay. To the west of Toronto are many charming small towns, such as Stratford, with its world-renowned Shakespearean theater festival, and the Mennonite community of St. Jacobs. Further west, along the shores of Lake Huron, sandy beaches stretching north and south of the lovely town of Goderich beckon. The Niagara Peninsula, south and east, can easily fill a weekend, with attractions such as Niagara Falls and Ontario's best wine country.

Bust of Shakespeare

BEYOND TORONTO

1 Top 10 Sights see pp101–103
1 Restaurants see p107
1 Wineries see p106
1 Shops see p105
1 Country Stays see p104

A horse-drawn carriage, a charming way to tour Niagara-on-the-Lake

① Niagara-on-the-Lake

MAP Q3 ■ Niagara Historical Museum: 43 Castlereagh St; 905 468 3912; open May–Oct: 10am–5pm daily; Nov–Apr: 1–5pm daily; adm

This historic town looks much as it did in the early to mid-1800s. Beautiful Georgian and Neo-Classical homes and charming shops reward leisurely exploration. History buffs won't want to miss the Niagara Historical Museum, with exhibits on the region's fascinating past. The town is a good base for excursions along the scenic Niagara Parkway and to wineries *(see p106)*. It is also home to the summer Shaw Festival.

② Niagara Falls

While the town itself sends kitsch to new heights, the falls *(see pp34–5)* are spectacular – truly a natural wonder and well worth the trip.

③ Stratford

MAP P2 ■ Stratford Perth Museum: 4275 Huron Rd; 519 393 5311; open May–Nov: 9am–5pm daily; adm; www.stratfordperthmuseum.ca

Globally known for its Shakespeare festival, the city continues the theme of the bard with, among other things, a garden planted with some species named in his plays. Check out local history at Stratford Perth Museum *(see p43)*, and the fine High Victorian Perth County Court House (1887).

④ Gravenhurst

MAP Q1 ■ Muskoka Steamships: www.realmuskoka.com ■ Bethune Memorial House: 235 John St N, Gravenhurst; 705 687 4261; www.pc.gc.ca/bethune

Gravenhurst is a good base from which to explore the Muskoka region. It is also the departure point for lake cruises aboard an 1887 steamship. Stretching from Algonquin Park to Georgian Bay, Muskoka has over 1,600 lakes and rivers, and beaches that offer swimming opportunities.

Gravenhurst, a pretty lakeside town

⑤ Royal Botanical Gardens

MAP P3 ■ 680 Plains Rd W, Burlington ■ Open 10am–dusk daily

Four gardens and acres of nature sanctuaries are replete with greenhouses and trails. The world's largest lilac collection blooms in spring, and centuries-old roses thrive summer to fall. In winter, visitors enjoy the indoor Mediterranean Garden.

Maple Syrup Museum, St. Jacobs

6 St. Jacobs and Elora
MAP P2

Arts and crafts, antiques, and gift shops set in 19th-century buildings; bakeries; and cozy restaurants abound in these historic villages. Craft and food vendors at St. Jacobs Farmers' Market (open year-round) include those offering the area's specialty, maple syrup, sold by local Mennonites. For more on this sweet treat, visit the Maple Syrup Museum at 1441 King Street N, St. Jacobs. A 15-mile (24-km) drive northeast is Elora, on the bank of the Grand River, and stunning Elora Gorge.

7 Georgian Bay Islands National Park
MAP P1 ■ DayTripper: 705 526 8907 (booking ahead recommended)

Georgian Bay's rugged landscape is characterized by the windswept rock and pines of the Canadian Shield. Thousands of islands are scattered across the Bay, and some 59 make up the park. Access to the largest, Beausoleil, with its hiking trails, sandy beaches, forest, and a variety of reptiles and amphibians, is via a 15-minute boat ride aboard the *DayTripper* from the town of Honey Harbour.

8 Goderich
MAP N2 ■ Huron County Museum: 110 North St; open Jan–Apr: 10am–4:30pm Tue–Fri (until 8pm Thu), 1–4:30pm Sat; May–Dec: 10am–4:30pm Tue–Sat (until 8pm Thu), 1–4:30pm Sun ■ Huron Historic Gaol: 181 Victoria St N; open May–Aug: 10am–4:30pm Mon–Sat, 1–4:30pm Sun; Sep & Oct: 1–4pm Sun–Fri, 10am–4:30pm Sat; adm ■ Marine Museum: open Jul & Aug: 1–4:30pm daily

Founded in 1827, this town on the shores of Lake Huron has a rich marine history and fine Victorian architecture. Its downtown streets radiate from an octagonal "square;" at its center is the Huron County Courthouse and Courthouse Park. The Huron County Museum has a fine collection of old farm equipment and military artifacts. Also of interest is the Huron Historic Gaol (built 1839–42) and the Marine Museum.

One of the tiny islands dotting Georgian Bay Islands National Park

⑨ Long Point Provincial Park

MAP P3 ▪ Hwy 59, 6 miles (10 km) south of Port Rowan ▪ 519 586 2133

This world-renowned refuge for migrating birds has been recognized by the United Nations as a biosphere reserve. Formed over thousands of years by sand washed from Lake Erie's shoreline, the 25-mile (40-km) sand spit has sand beaches and shallow waters. Spring and fall are idea for bird-watching; trails through dunes, forests, and wetlands can be enjoyed year-round. Camp sites have showers and electrical hook-ups.

A street in the heart of Collingwood

⑩ Collingwood

MAP P1 ▪ Blue Mountain Ski Resort: 705 445 0231 ▪ Scenic Caves Nature Adventures: 705 446 0256

This town takes full advantage of Niagara Escarpment scenery. A high point of the escarpment before it dips to Georgian Bay at Collingwood, nearby Blue Mountain is Ontario's best ski hill. At Scenic Caves Nature Adventures, walk Ontario's longest suspension footbridge or explore the limestone and ice caves.

A DRIVE IN THE COUNTRY

▶ MORNING

Start at **St. Jacobs Farmers' and Flea Markets**, admiring the handi-crafts, collectibles, and foodstuffs of over 600 vendors. After stocking up on snacks, walk across the parking lot to the **Trolley Shop** for a 75-minute horse-drawn trolley tour through Mennonite country *(open Apr–Oct)*.

After the tour, drive to the Visitor Centre at 1406 King Street N; it features a short video on Mennonite history, photo exhibits, and a replica of a Mennonite Meetinghouse. When ready for lunch, head to **Stone Crock** *(No. 1396)*, for a country-style buffet.

AFTERNOON

Drive east on County Road 17; in a few miles you'll come to Road 22. Turn north to Route 86, then east on 86, watching for the sign to West Montrose. In this small town, look for the last remaining covered bridge in Ontario – called the kissing bridge by locals. The bridge crosses Grand River, a Heritage Waterway. Take Route 23 (turning into R21) north to charming **Elora**, 10 minutes away.

Browse its craft and antiques shops and admire the old lime-stone buildings before walking to the Elora Gorge Conservation Area to swim, hike, and enjoy your picnic snacks by the water.

Dinner is just a short drive away. To dine at the 1860s **Breadalbane Inn** *(487 St. Andrew Street W)* head down Route 18 to Fergus, which is rich both in Scottish history and late 19th-century architecture.

See map on p100 ←

Shops

1 Farmers' Markets
www.farmersmarkets
ontario.com
June to October, usually on Saturday mornings, local farmers sell fresh produce – fiddleheads, white asparagus, wild blueberries and mushrooms, and much more – at over 148 markets throughout Ontario.

2 Ontario Wines
Try award-winning wines at vineyards (see p106) across the Niagara Peninsula before stocking up the cellar.

Greaves jam

3 Craft Beer
MAP P2 ■ Neustadt Springs: 456 Jacob St, Neustadt; 519 799 5790
Ontario's microbreweries have enjoyed continuous popularity. Many, such as Neustadt Springs, offer tastings and tours.

4 Quilts
MAP P2 ■ Mennonite Quilts: 1389 King St N, St. Jacobs; 519 664 1817
The best place to buy these durable and gorgeous covers is St. Jacobs, where local Mennonite women still practice the traditional craft of hand-quilting. Stop in at Mennonite Quilts.

5 Factory Outlets
MAP Q3 ■ Canada One: 7500 Lundy's Lane, Niagara Falls; 905 356 8989
Snap up bargains on brands such as Guess, Roots, and Nike at Niagara Falls' outlet stores.

6 Fruits and Preserves
MAP Q3 ■ Greaves Jams and Marmalades: 55 Queen St, Niagara-on-the-Lake; 1 800 515 9939
In summer and fall, roadside stands in the Niagara region sell luscious fruits. Local companies turn these into jams, which are available at select stores. Greaves preserves are especially popular.

7 Maple Syrup
The sap of Ontario's sugar maples is made into delicious pancake syrup and candies, sold at farmers' markets and shops.

8 Arts and Crafts
The work of Ontario's arts and crafts community – pottery, hand-blown glass, and jewelry – can be found across the province at fairs, markets, boutiques, and galleries.

9 Antiques
Hunting for vintage Canadian furniture, toys, silver, and china in Ontario towns is great sport. For a large selection, head to Erin, Jordan, St. Jacobs, Neustadt, and Elora.

10 Handmade Furniture
MAP P2
In southern Ontario, especially around Kitchener-Waterloo, Mennonite men craft durable country-style furniture from local woods. Watch for signs on the smaller roads pointing the way.

Mennonite quilter at work

See map on p100

Country Stays

 1 Langdon Hall Country House Hotel & Spa
MAP P2 ▪ 1 Langdon Dr, RR 3, Cambridge ▪ 1 800 268 1898 ▪ www.langdonhall.ca ▪ $$$

This hotel *(see p107)* has beautifully appointed rooms, lovingly tended gardens, a spa, and fine cuisine.

2 Prince of Wales Hotel
MAP Q3 ▪ 6 Picton St, Niagara-on-the-Lake ▪ 1 888 669 5566 ▪ www.vintage-hotels.com ▪ $$

Impeccable service, opulent rooms, a spa, and a wine list to match the fabulous cuisine at this historic hotel in the heart of town.

A bedroom at the Prince of Wales

3 The Little Inn at Bayfield
MAP N2 ▪ 26 Main St, Bayfield ▪ 1 800 565 1832 ▪ www.littleinn.com ▪ $$

This historic inn near Lake Huron, first opened in 1832 as a coach house, justifiably prides itself on its fine restaurant and spa. Country antiques decorate the rooms.

4 Hockley Valley Resort
MAP P2 ▪ RR 1, Orangeville ▪ 519 942 0754 ▪ www.hockley.com ▪ $$

Nestled in a valley, this resort is a perfect base for pursuing outdoor activities such as downhill or cross-country skiing, golfing, tennis, and hiking. There is also a good spa.

5 Sherwood Inn
MAP Q1 ▪ 1090 Sherwood Rd, Port Carling ▪ 866 844 2228 ▪ www.sherwoodinn.ca ▪ $$

On the shores of Lake Joseph, this hotel with cottages makes an ideal base for outdoor pursuits.

6 Inn on the Twenty
MAP Q3 ▪ 3845 Main St, Jordan ▪ 1 800 701 8074 ▪ www.innonthetwenty.com ▪ $$$

A luxurious inn with suites in the heart of Niagara wine country. Spa and winery packages are available.

7 Deerhurst Resort
MAP Q1 ▪ 1235 Deerhurst Dr, Huntsville ▪ 1 800 461 4393 ▪ www.deerhurstresort.com ▪ $$$

This lakeside resort and spa, set on 800 acres (325 ha) of Muskoka countryside, is suitable for families and couples.

8 The Oban Inn
MAP Q3 ▪ 160 Front St, Niagara-on-the-Lake ▪ 866 359 6226 ▪ www.obaninn.ca ▪ $$

Overlooking Lake Ontario and surrounded by lush gardens, this inn has beautiful rooms and a fine restaurant. Short walk to the town.

9 Benmiller Inn
MAP N2 ▪ 81175 Benmiller Rd ▪ 1 800 265 1711 ▪ www.benmillerinnandspa.com ▪ $$

Close to the beaches of Lake Huron, this inn combines country charm and elegance. There's a spa too.

10 The Westover Inn
MAP P2 ▪ 300 Thomas St, St. Mary's ▪ 519 284 2977 ▪ www.westoverinn.com ▪ $

In a quiet village, this Victorian house was once a seminary. It has comfortable rooms and extensive grounds.

For key to hotel prices see p116

Wineries

1 Vineland Estates Winery
MAP Q3 ▪ 3620 Moyer Rd, Vineland ▪ 1 888 846 3526

One of the most attractive wineries in the region, this vineyard has an 1857 stone carriage house, an excellent restaurant, and guided tours and tastings.

2 Fielding Estate
MAP Q3 ▪ 4020 Locust Lane, Beamsville ▪ 1 888 778 7758

Informative wine tours take guests into the vineyards, through the winery and up to the tasting room. The gorgeous patio boasts a stunning vista of Toronto in the distance.

3 Trius Winery at Hillebrand
MAP Q3 ▪ 1249 Niagara Stone Rd, Niagara-on-the-Lake ▪ 1 800 582 8412

Along with estate tours and tastings, Trius hosts events, such as jazz and blues shows, in July and August.

4 Peninsula Ridge Estates Winery
MAP Q3 ▪ 5600 King St W, Beamsville ▪ 905 563 0900

The winemaker, local boy Jamie Evans, creates interesting blends; the whites are especially good. The restaurant *(see p107)* is set in a lovely Victorian house.

5 Inniskillin Wines
MAP Q3 ▪ Line 3, Service Rd 66, Niagara-on-the-Lake ▪ 1 888 466 4754

One of Ontario's oldest quality vineyards, established in 1975 and famous for its icewines, has guided tours. The shop and tasting bar are in a renovated 1920s barn.

6 Jackson-Triggs Vinters
MAP Q3 ▪ 2145 Niagara Stone Rd, Niagara-on-the-Lake ▪ 905 468 4637

This winery is one of the most technologically advanced facilities in the region. Tours and tastings.

7 Thirty Bench Wine Makers
MAP Q3 ▪ 4281 Mountainview Rd, Beamsville ▪ 905 563 1698

This little winery is known for its small lot, limited-production wines. Tastings are held in a rustic building overlooking the vineyards.

8 Malivoire Wine Company
MAP Q3 ▪ 4260 King St E, Beamsville ▪ 1 866 644 2244

In a region known primarily for its white wines, this organic vineyard produces excellent reds. A tasting room is set amid production tanks.

9 Reif Estate Winery
MAP Q3 ▪ 15608 Niagara Pkwy, Niagara-on-the-Lake ▪ 905 468 7738

This family winery has 125 acres (51 ha) of scenic vineyards. The boutique's design is inspired by an 1870s coach house. Daily tours are held in summer, and visitors can also enjoy the Wine Sensory Garden.

10 Château des Charmes
MAP Q3 ▪ 1025 York Rd, Niagara-on-the-Lake ▪ 905 262 4219

This family vineyard boasts over seven generations of wine-growing experience, with grapes harvested exclusively from their vineyards. There is a tasting bar, shop, and splendid rose garden.

Château des Charmes

Restaurants

1 Eigensinn Farm
MAP P1 ▪ RR 2, Singhampton
▪ 519 922 3128 ▪ Closed L ▪ $$$

Intimately gathered in chef Michael Stadländer's farmhouse, diners feast on exquisite, organic courses. Prices reflect the exclusive setting.

2 13th Street Winery
MAP Q3 ▪ 1776 Fourth Ave, Stratford ▪ 905 984 8463 ▪ Closed D ▪ $$

House wines are paired with fresh seasonal dishes at this restaurant and winery. Lunch is served on the veranda, which overlooks the vines.

Dining room, Peller Estates Winery

3 Peller Estates Winery
MAP Q3 ▪ 290 John St E, Niagara-on-the-Lake ▪ 1 888 673 5537 ▪ $$$

Enjoy the enchanting vineyard view and take the tour before sitting down for a meal. Local and seasonal ingredients are used in the five- and seven-course tasting menus.

4 Langdon Hall
MAP P2 ▪ 1 Langdon Dr, RR 3, Cambridge ▪ 1 800 268 1898 ▪ $$

Chef Jason Bangerter produces sublime dishes from iconic Canadian ingredients. The stately mansion (see p104) might entice you to stay.

> **PRICE CATEGORIES**
> Price categories include a three-course meal for one, half a bottle of wine, and all unavoidable extra charges including tax.
> ....
> $ under $50 $$ $50–120 $$$ over $120

5 The Prune
MAP P2 ▪ 151 Albert St (Shaw Club Hotel), Stratford ▪ 519 271 5052 ▪ Closed late Nov–early Apr (call to check ahead of visit) ▪ $$

Canadian cuisine and outstanding wines. Diners decide the number of courses; the menu is fixed-price.

6 Tiara
MAP Q3 ▪ 155 Byron St, Niagara-on-the-Lake ▪ 905 468 2195 ▪ $$

Here savory roast and catch of the day join delights such as butter-poached lobster and rack-of-lamb.

7 The Kitchen House at Peninsula Ridge
MAP Q3 ▪ 5600 King St W, Beamsville ▪ 905 563 0900 ▪ Closed Mon & Tue ▪ $$

Experience fine dining in a brick home atop a hill. Part of the Peninsula Ridge Estates Winery (see p106).

8 Bijou
MAP P2 ▪ 105 Erie St, Stratford ▪ 519 273 5000 ▪ Closed Sun, Mon & Tue–Sat L ▪ $$

Quirky decor sets the stage for imaginative modern French dishes.

9 Zees Grill
MAP Q3 ▪ 92 Picton St, Niagara-on-the-Lake ▪ 905 468 5715 ▪ $$

The Niagara region is celebrated for its produce and wines, and Zees scores in both areas. There's a large patio, too.

10 Thyme on 21
MAP N2 ▪ 80 Hamilton St, Goderich ▪ 519 524 4171 ▪ Closed Mon & Tue ▪ $$

This unpretentious place is housed in a gorgeous Victorian home. The menu features traditional dishes.

See map on p100

Streetsmart

Flight Stop **by Michael Snow at the CF Toronto Eaton Centre**

Getting To and Around Toronto

Arriving by Air

Pearson International Airport is the arrival point for most international visitors. Lying 16 miles (26 km) northwest of downtown, it is Canada's largest and busiest airport. Those flying shorter distances by turboprop may land at the much smaller **Billy Bishop Toronto City Airport**, located on the Toronto Islands near downtown.

The **UPExpress** train from Pearson takes 25 minutes to reach Union Station and runs every 15 minutes between 5:30am and 1am. Buy the **Presto** travel card for discounts. Use of the card is often confusing even for locals, and procedures are different depending on the transit system and vehicle, so check online for instructions.

At Pearson, limousines (flat rate) as well as taxis (both flat rate and metered) are plentiful outside the arrivals area (avoid drivers who tout inside the airport, they are usually unlicensed). Buses run by TTC, GO Transit, and others offer connections to alternative destinations in the region.

Billy Bishop Airport is connected by a ferry, free shuttle bus, and pedestrian tunnel. Both airports have car-rental booths.

Arriving by Rail

Union Station is Toronto's principal train station, and a hub for trains to the US and other parts of Canada, the subway, and regional **GO Transit** (Government of Ontario) buses. **Amtrak** and **VIA Rail** are great for train travel in the region.

Arriving by Bus

Greyhound and **Megabus** provide long-distance, economical bus services between Toronto and other cities. They arrive at and depart from the **Toronto Coach Terminal**.

Getting Around by Public Transport

The **Toronto Transit Corporation (TTC)** runs a well-integrated network of subways, buses, and streetcars. A single fare covers a trip of any distance within Toronto city and includes transfers (an extra fare is required beyond the city limits). Day and family passes offer savings, depending on the number of trips. Check the TTC website for rates and schedules.

The GO Transit system is the regional service for the Greater Toronto and Hamilton area. It provides an excellent way to visit Niagara Falls, with direct trains on summer weekends, and a train-bus service at all other times.

Getting Around by Car

A driver's license valid in your own country is valid in Ontario for up to three months after you arrive. If you plan to stay longer, you will need to have an International Driver's Permit, which must be obtained in your home country before you arrive.

Insurance coverage for drivers is mandatory in Ontario; before leaving home, check your own policy to see if you are covered in a rental car. Most rental agencies will offer damage and liability insurance; it is a good idea to have both.

Toronto's roads are orderly but often they can get very congested (Hwy 401 is the busiest road in North America), and parking in the city is expensive, making public transport a better choice. Most city attractions are accessible by transit, but a car may be convenient for outlying places such as the beaches, and will be useful for day trips to other destinations outside the city.

Using a mobile phone while behind the wheel is against the law. It is also illegal to pass a stopped streetcar until the doors have closed. The **Drive in Ontario** website offers useful information for visitors who plan to navigate the city by car.

Getting Around by Taxi

Cabs can be flagged down on most main downtown streets. Visitors can also order a cab over the telephone. Rates and fares are set by the city. It is customary to tip the drivers, usually 15–20 per cent of the fare. Reliable cab companies include **Beck**, **Co-op**, **Crown**, and **Diamond**. **Uber** is a cheaper alternative.

Getting Around by Ferry

Ferries to the Toronto Islands depart from the foot of Bay Street. The trip is about 15 minutes. Get to the docks by taking the 509 Harbourfront or the 510 Spadina streetcar south to the Bay and Queens Quay stop, or the Bay bus No. 6 southbound from the corner of Front and Bay. Call or go online for **ferry schedules**.

Getting Around by Bicycle

Bike Share Toronto has sturdy rental bicycles stationed all over town. Pricing is economical if you make short trips between bike stations. If you keep the bike with you, extra fees quickly add up. Wearing a helmet is mandatory for children, but not for adults. Be wary of streetcar tracks, which can be a hazard.

Getting Around on Foot

Toronto is a walkable city. Streets are generally safe, and the grid layout makes navigation easy. In winter, escape the cold by going underground to the **PATH** system. Cross streets carefully at intersections or crosswalks, and be aware that drivers are permitted to turn right on a red light. They are supposed to yield right of way to pedestrians – but not all drivers do.

Bus and Boat Tours

CitySightseeing Toronto offers a combined boat and bus tour of downtown Toronto and the harbour. A combination deal adds Niagara Falls. Several companies, including **Get Your Guide**, **Toronto Harbour Cruises**, and **Toronto Tours** offer tours and cruises around the harbour and on Lake Ontario. It is also possible to book a day tour on board a three-masted schooner with **Tallship Cruises Toronto**.

DIRECTORY

ARRIVING BY AIR

Billy Bishop Toronto City Airport
w portstoronto.com/airport.aspx

Pearson International Airport
416 247 7678, 1 866 207 1690 (for information about flights)
w torontopearson.com

Presto
w prestocard.ca

UPExpress
w upexpress.com

ARRIVING BY RAIL

Amtrak
w amtrak.ca

GO Transit
w gotransit.com

VIA Rail
w viarail.ca

ARRIVING BY BUS

Greyhound
w greyhound.ca

Megabus
w ca.megabus.com

Toronto Coach Terminal
610 Bay St
w torontocoachterminal.com

GETTING AROUND BY PUBLIC TRANSPORT

Toronto Transit Corporation (TTC)
610 Bay St
w ttc.ca

GETTING AROUND BY CAR

Drive in Ontario
w ontario.ca/page/drive-ontario-visitors

GETTING AROUND BY TAXI

Beck
416 751 5555

Co-op
416 504 2667

Crown
416 240 0000

Diamond
416 366 6868

Uber
w uber.com/cities/toronto/

GETTING AROUND BY FERRY

Ferry Schedules
416 392 8193
w toronto.ca

GETTING AROUND BY BICYCLE

Bike Share Toronto
w bikesharetoronto.com

GETTING AROUND ON FOOT

PATH
w torontopath.com

BUS AND BOAT TOURS

CitySightseeing Toronto
w citysightseeingtoronto.com

Get Your Guide
w getyourguide.com

Tallship Cruises Toronto
w tallshipcruisestoronto.com

Toronto Harbour Cruises
w torontoharbour.com

Toronto Tours
w torontotours.ca

Practical Information

Passports and Visas

A valid passport, with a visa when needed, must be presented by visitors upon entry to Canada. US citizens, like all other visitors, must have a valid passport that extends beyond the duration of the trip. Residents of many countries, such as Australia, New Zealand, and the majority of European countries, do not need a visa for Canada, but they do need an online Electronic Travel Authorization (eTA). Visitors may remain in Canada for up to six months. The **Visit Canada** website has useful information on visas.

In Toronto, the **British Consulate-General**, **US Consulate-General**, and **Australian Consulate-General**, among others, can provide consular services to their nationals.

Customs and Immigration

Canada's rules governing what can be brought into the country are complex. In general, do not bring live animals, fresh fruit, vegetables, meat, dairy products, plants, or firearms into Canada without first obtaining authorization. Limited amounts of alcohol and tobacco may be imported duty-free by visitors who are of age (19 and 18 years old, respectively). Upon entry into Canada, if you are carrying any cash amount equal to or greater than $10,000, you must declare it.

Travel Safety Advice

Visitors can get up-to-date travel safety information from the **UK Foreign & Commonwealth Office**, the **US Department of State**, and the **Australian Department of Foreign Affairs and Trade**.

Health

Unless your own health insurance covers medical costs while traveling, buying comprehensive health and dental insurance is strongly advised. Canada does not provide medical services to visitors free of charge. Many credit card companies provide some degree of insurance; it is worthwhile checking this out before your trip.

Toronto does not pose many serious health hazards. However, the summer can be hot. Wear sunscreen. There are no venomous snakes in the Toronto area, and few dangerous insects, but mosquitoes are common and can be a nuisance in warm weather. Rabies outbreaks sometimes occur in Ontario. If you are bitten or scratched by an animal (domestic or wild), see a doctor immediately. The local wildlife usually stays away from humans, but it is best to keep your distance and don't touch any wild animals that seem "tame." If you visit forested or overgrown areas, watch out for giant hogweed and poison ivy, which can cause very painful blisters.

For minor ailments, pharmacists can be helpful. The majority of pharmacies are open from 9am to 9–10pm; some are open 24 hours a day. One of the most central is at **Shoppers Drug Mart** at Yonge and Carlton.

Hospitals in downtown Toronto include **Toronto General**, **St. Michael's**, **Mount Sinai**, the **Hospital for Sick Children**, and **Michael Garron Hospital**. Emergency treatment is available 24 hours a day.

For dental emergencies, the **Toronto Academy of Dentistry** emergency referral service links visitors with a nearby dentist after office hours. After midnight, go to an emergency room.

Personal Security

Toronto is generally safe, but visitors should always stay alert. Thieves may operate in crowded places. Pay attention to your surroundings and don't be distracted, especially if someone bumps into you. Don't carry more cash than you need and don't put your wallet in a back pocket. If you use a purse, ensure it closes tightly and remains in your sight. Be cautious at ATM machines. Watch your luggage carefully at airports, bus and train stations, and while checking in and out of hotels. Leave valuables in the hotel's safe.

Although the streets are generally safe, avoid dark places at night, especially if you are on your own. Carry a good map or GPS phone and check your route ahead of time. If you plan on returning late, make sure you have enough cash for a taxi.

Emergency Services

If an emergency takes place, call the emergency service numbers. The city has a standard number for **ambulance**, **fire**, and **police**, as well as a **Toronto Police (non-emergency)** number and a tele-communications number for those who are **hearing impaired**.

Travelers with Specific Needs

Bathrooms in some older buildings are often up or down stairs and not easily reachable. Accessible streetcars operate on the 510 Spadina and 509 Harbourfront routes. The subway is also accessible, with the availability of more elevators to platforms and fully accessible ticket gates. All TTC buses are equipped with a ramp at the front door and have the ability to kneel.

Currency and Banking

The unit of currency here is the Canadian dollar, which is divided into 100 cents. Coins are in denominations of 5, 10, and 25 cents, and 1 dollar (the loonie) and 2 dollars (the toonie). There is no 1 cent coin; change is rounded to the nearest 5 cents. Bank notes (bills) come in denominations of $5, $10, $20, $50, $100, and $500. Newer bills are plastic.

American coins will usually be accepted in shops, but will not work in any vending machines. Some shops will accept payment in US dollars as a courtesy, with an exchange rate shown at the till, however, the change will be given in Canadian currency.

The best rate is generally available at one of Toronto's many banks or from liquor or beer stores. Rates at airport exchange booths are relatively poor. Most bank, debit, and credit cards with security chips will work in Canada. Visa and MasterCard are more commonly accepted than American Express.

Canada's **Scotiabank** offers no-fee ATM withdrawals for customers of Westpac (Australia/NZ), Bank of America (US), Barclays (UK), and others.

DIRECTORY

PASSPORTS AND VISAS

Australian Consulate-General
W canada.embassy.gov.au

British Consulate-General
W ukincanada.fco.gov.uk

US Consulate-General
W ca.usembassy.gov

Visit Canada
W cic.gc.ca/english/visit

TRAVEL SAFETY ADVICE

Australian Department of Foreign Affairs and Trade
W dfat.gov.au
W smartraveller.gov.au

UK Foreign & Commonwealth Office
W gov.uk/foreign-travel-advice

US Department of State
W travel.state.gov

HEALTH

Hospital for Sick Children
555 University Ave
C 416 813 1500
W sickkids.ca

Michael Garron Hospital
825 Coxwell Ave
C 416 461 8272
W tegh.on.ca

Mount Sinai
600 University Ave
C 416 586 5054
W mountsinai.on.ca

Shoppers Drug Mart
465 Yonge St
C 416 408 4000
W shoppersdrugmart.ca

St. Michael's
30 Bond St
C 416 360 4000
W stmichaelshospital.com

Toronto Academy of Dentistry
C 416 967 5649
W tordent.com

Toronto General
200 Elizabeth St
C 416 340 3946
W uhn.ca

EMERGENCY SERVICES

Ambulance, Fire, Police
C 911

Hearing Impaired
C 416 467 0493

Toronto Police (non-emergency)
C 416 808 2222
W torontopolice.on.ca

CURRENCY AND BANKING

Scotiabank
W scotiabank.com

Telephone and Internet

Free Wi-Fi is available in most hotels and many restaurants and coffee shops across the city. Wireless Toronto is a non-profit community group bringing Wi-Fi to as many public spaces in Toronto as possible. Public telephones are becoming hard to find. Local calls cost 50 cents, and there is no limit on the duration of the call. For a long-distance number in North America, dial the prefix 1 and then the city code. To dial abroad, dial 011 + country code + city code.

Mobile phone services are expensive compared to the US and Europe, and are usually based around a long-term contract. However some providers, including **Fido** and **Koodo**, offer prepaid phone and Internet.

Check if your mobile phone provider offers service in Canada. For example, the UK's O2 and Orange networks work through Canada's **Rogers** network. If not, it may be possible to buy a prepaid SIM card before you come to Canada.

Postal Services

In Canada, post offices are normally located at a counter in pharmacies. However, you can often buy stamps at grocery stores and gas stations.

News and Media

Canada's main national newspaper is *The Globe and Mail*. The second-largest paper, with a more Toronto-centric slant, is the *Toronto Star*. Toronto weekly *Now* is available free at cafés, bars, bookstores, libraries, and street boxes throughout the city and is the best source for information on the local music and art scene. The monthly magazine *Toronto Life* is also helpful. Both are available online.

The national broadcaster **CBC** offers news on radio, TV, and its website. The popular **CBC Radio** gives a good feel for Canadian culture. For a sense of bustling Toronto, watch the news and magazine shows on **CityTV**.

Time Difference

Toronto is in the Eastern Standard Time (EST) zone (5 hours behind London, England). Clocks switch to Daylight Saving Time (an hour forward) from the second Sunday in March to the first Sunday in November.

Electrical Appliances

Canada's electrical supply conforms to the same standard used in the United States – 120 volts, 60 Hz. Many electronic devices will work with only a plug adapter. Other devices, such as hairdryers, may require a voltage converter. Converters are available at airports, train stations, and electronic stores, but research your requirements carefully before you leave home.

Weather

Its southern location and proximity to Lake Ontario make Toronto one of the warmer cities in Canada. Visitors are surprised by how hot and humid city summers can be. The sudden cooling in fall can produce spectacular changes in the colors of leaves (mid-October). In winter, temperatures often fall below freezing, and there can be snow and ice on the ground from December to March. Forecasts are usually in Celsius and in winter they will often include a "wind-chill" rating that factors in the extra cooling effect of wind on exposed skin.

Visitor Information

The **City of Toronto** and **Tourism Toronto** websites have useful information. Union Station has a visitor information booth, and also located here is the **Travellers' Aid Society. Ontariotravel.net**, the official tourism website for Ontario, offers information on Toronto, along with updates on local events. Many shopping malls have visitor information booths too.

Shopping

Most shops open 10am to 6pm, Monday to Saturday (often later on Thursday and Friday). Department stores and shops located in malls and commercial districts keep longer hours, from 10am to 9pm Monday to Saturday, and between noon and 5pm Sunday. Widely observed retail holidays in Canada are January 1, July 1, Labour Day, Thanksgiving, and Christmas. Prices on most goods are reduced dramatically on Boxing Day (December 26). Taxes are not included in the listed price unless specified, so it is best to always factor in an additional 13 per cent for HST (Harmonized Sales Tax). Items such as groceries are exempt from this tax.

Dining

Most restaurants take reservations. Mention if you have specific needs or dietary requirements. It is considered good form to cancel your reservation if your plans change.

Service charges and tips are not usually added to dining bills. For service at restaurants, cafés, and clubs, plan on tipping about 15 per cent of the pre-tax amount. At bars, leave a dollar or two for the bartender.

Breakfast is usually served in diners and coffee shops from about 6am to 10am. Lunch is available from about 11:30am to 2pm, and dinner between about 5pm and 10pm. Many restaurants and pubs offer a late-night menu. Brunches are often served on weekends only – and at some spots, on Sundays only – usually from 11am to 2pm or later. Some restaurants are closed on Sundays or Mondays, while others are closed on both days. Call ahead to check.

Drinking

The legal drinking age in the province of Ontario is 19. Ontario has very strict laws about drinking in public. Open bottles of alcohol are not allowed in public places. Fenced-off areas are set aside for selling and consuming

alcohol at large events. Sales of wine, spirits, and beer are restricted to **LCBO** (Liquor Control Board of Ontario) outlets, and beer and coolers to **The Beer Store**. Domestic wines are also sold in small wine stores and some supermarkets.

Smoking

Toronto is a smoke-free city except in designated areas, and smoking is outlawed in vehicles carrying passengers under 16 years.

Accommodation

Toronto's big hotels are pricey, but you may find some bargains using **Kayak** and **Expedia**. Downtown has various budget hotels. Toronto also has many **Airbnb** offerings (often condos) at much lower prices.

Accommodations in Ontario are taxed with a 13 per cent HST. An additional 3 per cent destination tax is also levied on some hotel rooms in the City of Toronto. The website of the **Canada Revenue Agency** offers more details on this.

Hotel rates can vary according to the hotel category, the day of the week, and the season. Peak rates are weekdays and April to December. Rack rates (the basic room rates) are used in this book to provide a guide price. It is almost always possible to get a better deal, especially if you book online.

Porters and bellhops are tipped at least $1 per bag or suitcase, and chambermaids a minimum of $2–3 per day ($5 in

high-end establishments). A hotel doorman will also appreciate a dollar or two for his services.

Places to Stay

PRICE CATEGORIES

For a standard double room per night (with breakfast if included), taxes, and extra charges.

$ under $175 $$ $175–350 $$$ over $350

Luxury Hotels

Delta Toronto Hotel

MAP K5 ▪ 75 Lower Simcoe St ▪ 416 849 1200 ▪ www.marriott. com ▪ $$

Set right in the heart of the Harbourfront district and connected to Union Station and the PATH system, this friendly and ultramodern hotel offers spectacular views of Lake Ontario and CN Tower. Amenities include a 24-hour gym, air conditioning and a play yard.

Fairmont Royal York

MAP K5 ▪ 100 Front St W ▪ 416 368 2511 ▪ www. fairmont.com/royal-york-toronto ▪ $$

Opposite Union Station, this large hotel has been a Toronto landmark since 1929. The magnificent lobby is a fitting backdrop for the heads of state who have stayed here. There are several restaurants and bars, including the cozy Library Bar (see p72), and a great spa.

The Omni King Edward Hotel

MAP L4 ▪ 37 King St E ▪ 416 863 9700 ▪ www. omnihotels.com/hotels/ toronto-king-edward ▪ $$

Opened in 1903, this grand hotel, affectionately called "the King Eddy," offers elegantly appointed rooms, courteous service, a spa, and every possible amenity guests may need.

Park Hyatt Toronto

MAP C3 ▪ 4 Avenue Rd ▪ 416 925 1234 ▪ www. toronto.park.hyatt.com ▪ $$

Luxurious, spacious rooms with marble bathrooms and free Wi-Fi, attentive service, and a central Yorkville location make this classy hotel a great favorite. The Hyatt's Roof Lounge (see p59) provides guests with a spectacular view of the city, and the posh Stillwater Spa is one of the city's best.

Ritz-Carlton Hotel

MAP J4 ▪ 181 Wellington St W ▪ 416 585 2500 ▪ www.ritzcarlton.com/ en/hotels/canada/toronto ▪ $$$

Set in the heart of the theater district, the Ritz-Carlton is a five-star hotel, and it overlooks the red carpet during the popular Toronto International Film Festival. It is known for pampering its guests, including children ("Ritz Kids"). The club-level rooms are luxurious.

Shangri-la Hotel

MAP K4 ▪ 188 University Ave ▪ 647 788 8888 ▪ www.shangri-la.com/ toronto/shangrila ▪ $$$

This luxurious hotel spans 17 floors and has a distinctly Asian aesthetic – raw silk wall coverings, a patio with a Japanese garden, and tea libraries. Rooms are exceptionally smart and modern.

Boutique Hotels

Broadview Hotel

MAP F4 ▪ 106 Broadview Ave ▪ 416 362 8439 ▪ www.thebroadview hotel.ca ▪ $$

Set in a meticulously restored 125-year-old Romanesque Revival building, this 58-room hotel boasts a grand facade and hip interior design.There is a café, a restaurant, and a rooftop bar with stunning views.

Gladstone Hotel

MAP K4 ▪ 1214 Queen St W ▪ 416 531 4635 ▪ www.gladstonehotel. com ▪ $$

The artist-designed rooms at this trendy, welcoming hotel are compact but comfortable. The hotel hosts arts events, and has a lively bar and café.

Madison Manor

MAP C3 ▪ 20 Madison Ave ▪ 416 922 5579 ▪ www.madisonmanor boutiquehotel.com ▪ $$

Featuring many unusual details, including alcove windows and fireplaces, this is a lovingly restored Victorian mansion. The Madison Manor aims to make its guests feel as though they have stepped into a picturesque English country inn.

The Old Mill Inn

MAP A2 ▪ 21 Old Mill Rd ▪ 416 236 2641 ▪ www.oldmilltoronto. com ▪ $$

This inn on the Humber River is a 15-minute drive west of Downtown (20 minutes by subway from Yonge and Bloor). All 44 rooms overlook the river and the 13 suites are located in the historic old mill building. All the rooms are spacious and luxurious, and there's a relaxing spa and rejuvenating wellness center, too.

The Hazelton

MAP C3 ▪ 118 Yorkville Ave ▪ 416 963 6300 ▪ www.thehazelton hotel.com ▪ $$$

A favorite with jetsetters, The Hazelton is Toronto's first five-star hotel and is located in the heart of upscale Yorkville. It features glamorous Hollywood-style rooms and a bar, which is great for spotting celebrities while sipping on cocktails.

SoHo Metropolitan

MAP J4 ▪ 318 Wellington St W ▪ 416 599 8800 ▪ www.metropolitan. com/soho ▪ $$$

Lovers of luxury will adore this boutique hotel in the Entertainment District. Duvets, walk-in closets, extravagant bathrooms with heated marble floors, and many high-tech gadgets are available as standard.

Windsor Arms

MAP C3 ▪ 18 Thomas St ▪ 416 971 9666 ▪ www. windsorarmshotel.com ▪ $$$

Personal service is writ large in this elegant hotel with just 28 guest rooms on the first four floors of a 14-story building. Guests enjoy the two-floor spa and delight in the cuisine of Courtyard Café. There is also a popular steakhouse and tearoom.

Business-Friendly Hotels

The Suites at One King West

MAP K4 ▪ 1 King St W ▪ 416 548 8100 ▪ www. onekingwest.com ▪ $

Located in the Financial District, this hotel is uniquely built atop a 1914 building that once housed the Dominion Bank of Canada. The hotel has a 24-hour business center, bistro, and private club. The views are amazing.

DoubleTree by Hilton Hotel Toronto Downtown

MAP K3 ▪ 108 Chestnut St ▪ 416 977 5000 ▪ www. doubletree3.hilton.com ▪ $$

Contemporary decor and luxurious touches pamper travelers. Restaurants Lai Wah Heen (see p56) and Hemispheres add to the pleasure of a stay here.

Hilton Toronto

MAP K4 ▪ 145 Richmond St W ▪ 416 869 3456 ▪ www3.hilton.com ▪ $$

In the financial district, this business hotel has spacious standard rooms, suites ideal for longer stays, and executive rooms with extras such as special work chairs.

InterContinental Toronto Centre

MAP J5 ▪ 225 Front St W ▪ 416 597 1400 ▪ www. torontocentre.inter continental.com ▪ $$

Attached to Toronto's Convention Centre, this hotel provides attentive service and excellent business facilities. The eighth floor is for Priority Club business guests.

Sheraton Centre

MAP K4 ▪ 123 Queen St W ▪ 416 361 1000 ▪ www. marriott.com ▪ $$

Steps from City Hall, this hotel complex bustles with conventioneers and tour groups. There are 1,377 rooms and good, efficient service.

Toronto Marriott Downtown Eaton Centre

MAP K3 ▪ 525 Bay St ▪ 416 597 9200 ▪ www. marriott.com ▪ $$

Featuring a full business center with secretarial service, dedicated business guestrooms, and 18 meeting rooms, this 18-story hotel is conveniently located next to the CF Toronto Eaton Centre (see pp30–31).

Westin Bristol Place Toronto Airport

MAP A2 ▪ 950 Dixon Rd ▪ 416 675 9444 ▪ www. westintorontoairport. com ▪ $$

Just five minutes from Pearson Airport, the hotel surprises at check-in with a waterfall in its lobby. Guests appreciate the modern, spacious rooms, personalized service, fitness center, indoor pool, and other amenities.

Westin Harbour Castle

MAP K6 ▪ 1 Harbour Sq ▪ 416 869 1600 ▪ www. marriott.com ▪ $$

With a location right on Lake Ontario, yet close to downtown, this high-rise hotel offers stunning views from its ample rooms. Facilities include a pool, fitness room, outdoor tennis court, spacious meeting rooms, and full business service.

For a key to hotel price categories see p116

Mid-Range Hotels

Eaton Chelsea
MAP L2 ■ 33 Gerrard St W
■ 416 595 1975 ■ www.
chelseatoronto.com ■ $$
Canada's biggest hotel,
with 1,590 guest rooms,
the Eaton Chelsea caters
equally well to business
travelers and families. An
indoor waterslide, the Kid
Centre, a teen lounge with
Xboxes, and a pool table
go a long way to keeping
all ages amused.

Hotel Victoria
MAP L4 ■ 56 Yonge St
■ 416 363 1666 ■ www.
hotelvictoria-toronto.
com ■ $$
Steps from Union Station
in the city's Financial
District, this 56-room
hotel offers excellent
service. It is located close
to many top attractions.

Hyatt Regency Toronto
MAP J4 ■ 370 King St W
■ 416 343 1234 ■ www.
torontoregency.hyatt.
com ■ $$
This extensively renovated
hotel is situated close to
the city's Entertainment
District. The rooms, fitted
with modern amenities,
look out over Downtown
Toronto and Lake Ontario.

International Plaza Hotel
MAP A2 ■ 655 Dixon Rd
■ 416 244 1711 ■ www.
marriott.com ■ $$
Near Pearson Airport, this
hotel has 433 guestrooms.
A variety of restaurants
and cafés, along with a
spa, a fitness center, and
an indoor swimming pool
with waterslides, ensure
you rarely need leave the
premises. Also a popular
conference center.

Novotel Toronto Centre
MAP L5 ■ 45 The
Esplanade ■ 416 367 8900
■ www.novotel.com ■ $$
Well placed near many
downtown attractions,
this Novotel is a good
example of the French
chain. The large rooms
are functional, and there
is a lovely lobby, fitness
room, and indoor pool.

Radisson Plaza Hotel Admiral Toronto Harbourfront
MAP J6 ■ 294 Queens
Quay W ■ 416 203 3333
■ www.radisson.com ■ $$$
Bright, large rooms in
this hotel, steps from
Lake Ontario and
harbourfront attractions,
appeal to both business
and leisure travelers
alike. There is a good
restaurant, and a roof-
top pool and deck that
overlooks the lake.

Budget Hotels and Accommodations

Bond Place Hotel
MAP D4 ■ 65 Dundas St E
■ 416 362 6061 ■ www.
bondplace.ca ■ $
Ideally located right in
the heart of Downtown
Toronto, Bond Place Hotel
is close to the CF Toronto
Eaton Centre, the theater
district, and many other
local attractions. The
rooms are modern and
well equipped, and the
hotel has a restaurant.

Hostelling International Niagara Falls
MAP Q3 ■ 4549 Cataract
Ave, Niagara Falls ■ 905
357 0770 ■ www.hi
hostels.ca/en ■ $
Located just a short
walk away from the

Niagara Falls, this
hostel is especially well
kept. There are a few
private rooms, along
with dorms and some
four-bed rooms. How-
ever, there are no private
baths in the rooms.

Hostelling International Toronto
MAP L4 ■ 76 Church St
■ 416 971 4440 ■ www.
hihostels.ca ■ $
Located just south of the
LGBT-oriented village,
this hostel provides one
of the city's cheapest
stays, with mainly shared
rooms in dorms. A few
private rooms with en
suite are also available.

Marriott Gateway on the Falls
MAP Q3 ■ 6755 Fallsview
Blvd, Niagara Falls ■ 1 800
618 9059 ■ www.marriott.
com ■ $
The comfortable rooms
in this high-rise hotel
offer glorious views of
the Niagara Falls. Hotel
staff are extremely helpful
and knowledgeable, and
the rooms are large and
well appointed.

Neill-Wycik College Hotel
MAP M2 ■ 96 Gerrard
St E ■ 416 977 2320
■ www.neill-wycik.
com ■ $
This student residence
turns into a guesthouse
from early May to the
end of August. While
the rooms are spartan
and the bathrooms are
shared, the price is right
for tight budgets. Groups
are welcome. The central
location means many of
the city's top destinations
are in walking distance.
Breakfast is included
in the price of the room.

The Planet Traveler Hostel

MAP H2 ▪ 357 College St ▪ 647 352 8747 ▪ www.theplanettraveler.com ▪ $

Housed in a 100-year-old building, this spacious, clean and conveniently located accommodation is one of Canada's greenest hostels. It also has a rooftop bar.

Victoria's Mansion Inn and Guest House

MAP L1 ▪ 68 Gloucester St ▪ 416 921 4625 ▪ www.victoriasmansion.com ▪ $

On a tree-lined street in the heart of Toronto's LGBT-oriented Village, this charming small hotel, with a lovely Victorian-style garden, provides a respite from the bustle of the city. All rooms come with private baths, and suites are equipped with a fridge and microwave. Free parking.

Victoria University

MAP D3 ▪ 140 Charles St W ▪ 416 585 4524 ▪ www.vicu.utoronto.ca ▪ $

Located on the campus of the University of Toronto, Victoria University opens its doors to budget travelers during summer-semester holidays from mid-May to the end of August. A quiet setting combined with a central location make these lodgings an excellent base from which to explore the city.

Cambridge Suites

MAP L4 ▪ 15 Richmond St E ▪ 416 368 1990 ▪ www.cambridgesuites toronto.com ▪ $$

Excellent service is standard at this hotel, which offers two-room

suites only. The fully equipped work areas have all the bells and whistles. A microwave, fridge, and coffee machine in every suite ensure you have all you need for your stay.

B&Bs

Annex Garden B&B

MAP B3 ▪ 445 Euclid Ave ▪ 416 258 1179 ▪ www.annexgarden.com ▪ $

Stay in a historic house in Little Italy, an unbeatable location. Two apartments and two rooms are available in this spiffy home that boasts four fireplaces and underfloor heating.

By the Park Bed & Breakfast

MAP A2 ▪ 92 Indian Grove ▪ 416 520 6102 ▪ www.bythepark.ca ▪ $

In this restored 1910 home, rooms are large and bathrooms are luxurious. You can unwind in the beautiful garden or warm up by one of the fireplaces, depending on the season. The price includes a delicious home-cooked vegan or vegetarian breakfast.

Downtown Home Inn

MAP D3 ▪ 2 Monteith St ▪ 1 877 271 0182 ▪ www.downtownhomeinn.com ▪ $

Located in a cul-de-sac, Downtown Home Inn is within walking distance of Yonge and Bloor street, at the crossroads of the city and subway system. Guests can kick back and relax in an elegantly furnished and airy historic brick home. This hotel provides all the modern amenities such as central AC, heating, TVs and Wi-Fi.

Making Waves Boatel

MAP H6 ▪ 539 Queens Quay W ▪ 647 403 2764 ▪ www.boatel.ca ▪ $

Be lulled to sleep in the lap of Lake Ontario. Set right in the Harbourfront marina, this moored boat has two cabins with a shared bath, and a larger stateroom with private bath. Enjoy evening drinks under the stars on the Sky Lounge.

McGill Inn

MAP L2 ▪ 110 McGill St ▪ 416 351 1503 ▪ www.mcgillbb.com ▪ $

Reasonable prices and eight tastefully decorated rooms, some with shared baths, and make this B&B in a restored Victorian townhouse a good choice for the budget-conscious traveler. It is a 10-minute walk away from the CF Toronto Eaton Centre.

Pimblett's Downtown Toronto B&B

MAP E4 ▪ 242 Gerrard St E ▪ 416 921 6898 ▪ $

The five cozy rooms in this Victorian house are decorated with all things British, such as antiques and bric-a-brac. It offers an eccentric stay in Cabbagetown. The owner, amuses guests with impressions of the Queen of England.

Smiley's B&B

MAP D6 ▪ 4 Dacotah Ave ▪ 416 203 8599 ▪ www.eralda.ca ▪ $

Snuggle up in the rooftop Belvedere Room of this Algonquin Island cottage. Have breakfast with your hosts, appreciate the tranquility, and explore Toronto Islands. A studio that sleeps four is available in summers.

For a key to hotel price categories see p116

General Index

Acknowledgments

Author

Lorraine Johnson is the author of several books and co-author of DK's Eyewitness Guide to Chicago. She lives in Toronto.

Barbara Hopkinson is a Toronto-based writer and editor who has directed a wide range of international projects.

Additional contributor
Dan Liebman

Publishing Director Georgina Dee

Publisher Vivien Antwi

Design Director Phil Ormerod

Editorial Ankita Awasthi Tröger, Avanika, Rachel Fox, Maresa Manara, Sally Schafer, Jackie Staddon, Rachel Thompson

Cover Design Maxine Pedliham, Vinita Venugopal

Picture Research Susie Peachey, Ellen Root, Lucy Sienkowska

Cartography Dominic Beddow, Simonetta Giori, Mohammad Hassan, Casper Morris

DTP Jason Little

Production Poppy Werder-Harris

Factchecker Taraneh Jerven

Proofreader Clare Peel

Indexer Helen Peters

First edition created by International Book Productions Inc., Toronto

Revisions Nayan Keshan, Sumita Khatwani, Shikha Kulkarni, Bandana Paul, Beverly Smart, Priyanka Thakur, Stuti Tiwari, Tanveer Zaidi

Commissioned Photography Rough Guides / Enrique Uranga

Picture Credits

The publisher would like to thank the following for their kind permission to reproduce their photographs:
Key: a-above; b-below/bottom; c-centre; f-far; l-left; r-right; t-top

123RF.com: Lin Chu-Wen 75cra; yelo34 66tl.

Adelaide Hall/Strut Entertainment: Matt Vardy 59tr.

Agha Khan Museum: Janet Kimber 61cl, 96b; Tom Arban Photography 43cl.

Alamy Stock Photo: All Canada Photos 51tl / Klaus Lang 4clb, 30–31, / Rolf Hicker 35tl; Jon Bilous 22–3; Bill Brooks 17tl, 19tl, 19clb; Lorne Chapman 3tl, 64–5; Cosmo Condina North America 35cr; Gaertner 13bl, 104bl; Bert Hoferichter 18c; Nick Jene 59clb; lucky-photographer 4t; maximimages.com 68cla; Jill Morgan 10crb; National Geographic Creative / Richard Nowitz 16cb; Nikreates 33bl; REUTERS / Roger Bacon 62br; Andrew Rubtsov 14cl; adiseshan shankar 15tr; Rosemarie Stennull 69cl, 102–3; Torontonian 3tr, 108–9; Arsalan Uljamil 35clb; Janusz Wrobel 45tr.

ALO Restaurant: 56bl.

Art Gallery Of Ontario: 4cr, 20clb.

Aunties & Uncles: 56ca.

AWL Images: Alan Copson 34bl.

Bridgeman Images: Art Gallery of Ontario, Toronto, Canada / *Eve* (c.1883) by Auguste Rodin10bl, / *Figure with Ulu* (1966) by Aqjangajuk Shaa, 20br, / *Autumn Leaves, Batchewana, Algoma* (c.1919) by James Edward Hervey Macdonald 20–21; *Venus Simultaneous* (1962) by Michael Snow 21tl, / *The Concert* (1918–19) by Pierre Auguste Renoir 21cr, / *Hina and Fatu* (c.1892) by Paul Gauguin 74tr.

Buca/Gab Communications: Rick O'Brien 83b.

Buddies in Bad Times Theatre: 55b.

Cafe é Diplomatico/Branding and Buzzing: 82tr.

Caffe Furbo: Kevin Bonnici 27bl.

Canada Opera Company: Sam Javanrouh 53cl.

Canada's Wonderland: 95tr; Graig Abel 50b.

The Ceili Cottage: 92cra.

CF Toronto Eaton Centre: 11cr.

Château des Charmes: 106b.

City Of Toronto Historic Sites: 78cra, 86tl, 94tl, 78cra; Summer Leigh Photography 68b.

Coal Miner's Daughter: 80br.

Courtesy of the Thomas Fisher Rare Book Library, University of Toronto: 60tl.

courtesy of Design Exchange: 70t.

Drake Hotel Properties: 81cr.

Dreamstime.com: Alexsvirid 49b; Amarita 57br; Appalachianviews 31tl, 46cla, 46–7bc, 48bl, 87tl; Artemzavarzin 16–17; Jon Bilous 7tr; Bokdavid 37bl; Canadapanda 63clb; Catstail 49cr; Chrisstanley 4cla; Clivechilvers 63br; Cpqnn 2tl, 8-9 ; Daddiomanottawa 36cla; Elenathewise 4cl, 103cl; Erandalx 45bl; Fabry10 17cl; Flusvarghi 98b; Harryfn 44bl; Roxana Gonzalez 95br; Iwhitwo 101t; Javenlin1018 15b, 24cl; Koco77 30clb; Lagron49 50ca; Lester69 60b; Chu-wen Lin 7br; Maudern 44t; Mikecphoto 18br, 36bc; Milosk50 41cl; Mishkaki 10cl; Noodles73 43tr; Pixart 11br; Rabbit75 34–5; Manon Ringuette 4crb; Ronniechua 4b, 77bl; Sampete 16cl, 31bl, 78bl; Camille Tsang 11br; Vdvtut 61tr; Vitaldrum 11tl; Wickedgood 47tr; Yelo34 12–13, 13cra.

El Catrin/Distillery Restaurants Corporation: 93cr.

Gadabout: Charlotte Giacomelli 91clb.

Gardiner Museum: Melissa Shimmerman 42ca.

Getty Images: Education Images 102tl; William England 37bl; EyeEm / Brady Baker 1; Rick Gerharter 54clb; FilmMagic / Jason LaVeris 41tr; LightRocket / Roberto Machado Noa 76cb, / Wolfgang Kaehler 100tl; Panoramic Images 76t; Brian Summers 87crb; Toronto Star / Todd Korol 89clb.

Greaves Jams: 104ca.

Harbourfront Centre: 67cra.

Hockey Hall of Fame: 32clb; AJ Messier Photography 32–3, 33cr.

iStockphoto.com: bakerjarvis 88t; Kenneth Cheung 19cla; JavenLin 2tr, 38–9; Orchidpoet 84–5, 101clb.

Julie's Cuban: Parisa Almasi 82clb.

Le Sélect Bistro: 56b.

Legoland Discovery Centre/Enterprise Canada: 97cla.

Liberty Group: 10br; Lorne Chapman 24br, 24–5, 25tl, 25crb.

Lula Lounge: 58t.

Marben: Rick O'Brien 73cla.

McMichael Canadian Art Collection: 96c.

Mercatto Restaurant Group: 73crb.

Mirvish.com: Edward Burtynsky 71cr; Paul Coltas 71bl.

Morba: 80ca.

National Ballet of Canada: *Elena Lobsanova and Guillaume Côté in Romeo and Juliet* photo Bruce Zinger 53tr.

NXNE Festival/Flip Publicity: 62t.

Old Spaghetti Factory: 51br.

images courtesy of Oliver & Bonacini Restaurants: Cindy La 99crb.

Omni King Edward Hotel: 92bl.

Ontario Heritage Trust: Peter Lusztyk 52t.

Ontario Science Centre: 42–3b.

The Oxley Public House/Broadcloth Hospitality: 81tr.

Peller Estates Winery and Restaurant: Cosmo Condina 107clb.

Prince of Wales Hotel/Vintage Hotels: 105cl.

Pusateri's Fine Foods: 79cb.

Rex by Shutterstock: Granger 40tl

Ripley's Aquarium of Canada: 6cla, 11cla, 28cl, 28crb, 29cr, Michael Hope 28–9, 29br.

Robert Harding Picture Library: Jean B. Heguy 67br.

Roots: 79tr.

Rouge National Urban Park: Parks Canada 98tl, / M Ruston 47cl.

Royal Ontario Museum: 10cra, 12clb; Brian Boyle 14tc.

St. Lawrence Market Complex: City Of Toronto / Jose San Juan 90t.

The Chase: Brandon Barre 57tl, 72b.

The Royal Conservatory: Tom Arban 52bl.

Tourism Toronto: Marketing Department of the The Distillery Historic District 26–7.

Young Centre for the Performing Arts: Tom Arban 27tl.

Cover

Front and spine: **Getty Images:** EyeEm / Brady Baker.

Back: **123RF.com:** Diego Grandi cla, Suranga Weeratunga tl; **Getty Images:** EyeEm / Brady Baker b; **SuperStock:** crb, Henry Georgi / All Canada Photos tr.

Pull Out Map Cover

Getty Images: EyeEm / Brady Baker.

All other images © Dorling Kindersley

For further information see: www.dkimages.com

As a guide to abbreviations in visitor information blocks: **Adm** *= admission charge;* **D** *= dinner;* **L** *= lunch.*

MIX
Paper from
responsible sources
FSC
www.fsc.org   FSC™ C018179

Penguin
Random
House

Printed and bound in China

First Edition 2012

Published in Great Britain by
Dorling Kindersley Limited
80 Strand, London WC2R 0RL

Published in the United States by
DK US, 1450 Broadway, Suite 801,
New York, NY 100018, USA

Copyright © 2005, 2020
Dorling Kindersley Limited

A Penguin Random House Company

19 20 21 22 10 9 8 7 6 5 4 3 2 1

**Reprinted with revisions 2007,
2009, 2011, 2013, 2015, 2018, 2020**

Published in Great Britain by Dorling Kindersley Limited.

A CIP catalog rerecord is available from the British Library.

A catalog record for this book is available from the Library of Congress.

ISSN 1479-344X

ISBN 978-0-2414-1043-1

Toronto Sight Index

Toronto Selected Street Index